Early Years Movement Skills
Description, Diagnosis and Intervention

N

Early Years Movement Skills

Description, Diagnosis and Intervention

MARY CHAMBERS EdD

and

DAVID SUGDEN PhD

University of Leeds

W

WHURR PUBLISHERS

LONDON AND PHILADELPHIA

Other Wiley Editorial Offices

John Wiley & Sons Inc., 111 River Street, Hoboken, NJ 07030, USA

Jossey-Bass, 989 Market Street, San Francisco, CA 94103-1741, USA

Wiley-VCH Verlag GmbH, Boschstr. 12, D-69469 Weinheim, Germany

John Wiley & Sons Australia Ltd, 42 McDougall Street, Milton, Queensland 4064, Australia

John Wiley & Sons (Asia) Pte Ltd, 2 Clementi Loop #02-01, Jin Xing Distripark,
Singapore 129809

John Wiley & Sons Canada Ltd, 22 Worcester Road, Etobicoke, Ontario, Canada M9W 1L1

Wiley also publishes its books in a variety of electronic formats. Some content that
appears in print may not be available in electronic books.

A catalogue record for this book is available from the British Library

ISBN -13   978-1-86156-498-6
ISBN -10   1-86156-498-8

Printed and bound in Great Britain by TJ International Ltd, Padstow, Cornwall

This book is printed on acid-free paper responsibly manufactured from sustainable
forestry in which at least two trees are planted for each one used for paper production.

Contents

Preface

Movement is a fundamental component of human life with the ability to make precise controlled movements being so much part of daily living. The conduct of countless acts becomes so automatic that they scarcely intrude upon consciousness and as such we often forget their diversity, richness and functional importance. It is hoped that by the time children reach school age they have built up a repertoire of skills that enable them to function effectively in the classroom and playground. However, some children on entry into school for some reason do not have a full range of these fundamental skills, obviously lacking in the abilities necessary for them to cope with the demands of the school environment. For some, this could be a direct result of lack of experience, while for others it could be a far more complex problem with potential long-term consequences. This lack of competence in motor skills often affects their academic work and their normal activities of daily living.

The period from 2 to 7 years of age is generally recognized as a time of acquisition of a number of fundamental motor skills leading to the development of a large repertoire of movement skills; that is those skills that are the building blocks for the functional movements they use throughout their lives. By six years of age a normally developing child will have in place a full range of fundamental movement skills including running, jumping, hopping, skipping, climbing, throwing, catching, kicking, striking, manipulating, writing and drawing. These skills will not necessarily be performed in a competent manner but the rudiments are there to be developed through refinement, combination, adaptation and exploration. If the fundamental skills are not developed in these years, problems may occur later and consequently on entry into school the child displaying difficulties may not be able to participate fully in classroom and playground activities. In addition, there is evidence that poor motor development can affect other areas of school activity including underachievement at school, lack of concentration, behaviour problems, low self-esteem, poor social competence and lack of physical hobbies. In general, the long-term prognosis for children with difficulties with motor skills who do not receive help is not good. This is particularly true if specific intervention is not given. When intervention is given the results are encouraging but for intervention to be effective, children need to be accurately and consistently identified and assessed.

This text begins with an overview of motor development and change, noting individual changes across the lifespan in the motor domain. The chapter examines types of change whilst also examining explanations of change including traditional theories, dynamical systems and ecological approaches. Chapter 2 describes the nature of change in the development of movement skills during the first seven years of life. The chapter is divided into two sections: the first section looks at motor development from birth to two years of age, examining reflexes and spontaneous movements before moving on to a more detailed analyses of descriptions of change in postural control, locomotion and manual control. The second section of the chapter is concerned with motor development from two to seven years of age, examining the functional motor skills which are necessary for engaging in functional, self-help and recreational everyday activities. It discusses the development of body control as seen in walking, running, jumping, hopping, throwing, balancing; manual skills and spatial and temporal accuracy.

Chapter 3 outlines difficulties children have with movement, specifically developmental coordination disorder (DCD); discussing the historical perspective, terminology, core characteristics, prevalence and the nature of DCD. Within this there is a discussion of possible sub types of DCD. There follows a section on the development of DCD through childhood, considering development in the early years and development from the early school years to adolescence. Finally, there is a section on associated and comorbid difficulties including a consideration of some of the more usual developmental disabilities which can co-exist with DCD.

Chapter 4 discusses the assessment of young children with movement difficulties, considering the uses and types of assessment and noting examples of current assessment instruments for the early years with particular discussion of context and assessment and underlying principles. The major part of the chapter is given to the development of the Early Years Movement Skills Checklist (EYMSC), describing the rationale and development, charting the various stages of construction. This is a unique instrument aimed specifically at assessing movement difficulties in children three to six years of age. The motor component of the checklist is discussed in depth with particular attention given to the chosen format of four sections (self-help skills, desk skills, general classroom skills and recreational/playground skills). The final part of the chapter briefly describes a study carried out to determine the reliability and validity of the Checklist.

Having detailed the assessment procedures to identify children with DCD, Chapter 5 deals with the management of the condition in the early years. A fundamental part of the assessment procedure is that children are accurately assessed which then leads to effective intervention. The first section outlines the concerns the condition reveals and is followed by a detailed section on how to obtain help. This section examines treatment options in education and health, giving particular attention to the Special Education Needs Code of Practice. A section follows on the principles and general guidelines for intervention discussing such principles as expert 'scaffolding', knowing and doing and priorities. The following section of the chapter gives specific guidelines for working at home and at school; activities discussed concern manual skills including self-help skills and handwriting, fundamental (gross motor) skills with suggested activities for throwing and catching, and general fundamental skills. A final section discusses the notion of a 'developmental coach' – with the suggestion that parents and carers are the most appropriate individuals to fulfil this role, ensuring that intervention should be a normal part of everyday life. Addresses and suggestions of other sources of help are given at the end of the chapter.

Finally, two appendices are presented. Appendix 1 is concerned with the technical information of the EYMSC; it details an investigation using the EYMSC to identify children with movement skills difficulties. The results and analysis section discusses the 426 Checklists in the main sample reporting on the interaction between the four sections of the Checklist and gender and the interaction of the four sections and age. Reliability coefficients are reported for interrater reliability and test-retest reliability followed by an examination of the stability of the checklist scores in the reliability study. A validity study of the EYMSC was also carried out and the results are reported with particular attention given to the predictive validity. Specificity and sensitivity measures are also reported. The discussion section concentrates on the validity and reliability of the checklist and performance differences between different ages and gender.

Appendix 2 contains the Early Years Movement Skills Checklist, along with instructions for the administration and interpretation of scores. This section can be photocopied. The following section contains activities for the motor skills described in earlier chapters and includes suggestions for manual skills, handwriting, balance, agility and ball skills.

Mary Chambers
David Sugden

Acknowledgements

There are a number of people we would like to thank for their help during the writing of this book. Firstly, we would both like to express our sincere thanks to the headteachers, teachers and children who so willingly participated in the research investigation during the development of the Early Years Movement Skills Checklist; without their hospitality, patience and kind co-operation our task would have been far more difficult.

Mary Chambers would also like to express her debt and gratitude to her family for their support and encouragement; her love and thanks go to her husband, Mark, especially for his words of advice and encouragement while writing this book. She would like to dedicate her efforts to her children JJ and Matt with her love and thanks to both of them.

David Sugden would like to dedicate his efforts to his children Rachel and Chris who constantly delight and surprise him.

CHAPTER 1

Motor development and change

Introduction

Development is a process through which the individual changes across the lifespan in a number of modalities such as cognitive, sensory, language, social and physical. These changes come in a number of different guises, some of them being very obvious and seen every day such as language development, others being less visible such as the development of moral behaviour which often requires a closer examination to detect change.

The motor domain is one in which changes are obvious and often dramatic, particularly early in life when motor responses are the dominant ones in the young infant. Like other areas of development, motor development is a change, and this change is related to the functional capacity of the individual to perform movement tasks. As a result of this change in functional capacity, the movement behaviour of the individual often changes if in a context that affords a change. A cautionary note should be inserted concerning physical growth which is often used simultaneously with motor development. It is indeed a part of motor development but only a part and this book alludes to physical growth as an independent variable or a constraint that will have an effect on our main focus, that of skilled coordinated movement. In a similar vein, age should not be directly equated with change in a linear manner; age is a variable that affects change, but not only varies by individual but also does so in a non-linear manner where step changes and plateaus are common.

There are many types of change that lead to different functional performance in children leading not only to individual change: the transaction with the environmental context also undergoes a transformation. Consider the variables in Figure 1.1.

This is a modification of a figure first proposed by Keogh and Sugden (1985) and describes the interplay of the *mover* and the *environmental context* and a related *movement task*. Environmental context and task

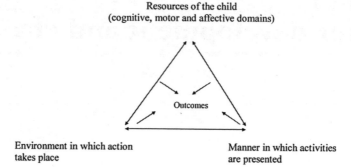

Figure 1.1 Interaction of the child, the environment and activities.

requirements are balanced against the individual mover resources to create a level of individual demand for any given situation. Keogh and Sugden (1985) note

> All parts of the movement situation change in relation to one another, making movement development into a series of transactional changes among mover, environments, and task ... (pp. 14–15)

In a similar vein, Newell (1986) made use of three similar variables in his paper examining constraints in motor behaviour. Thus, his constraints of environment, task and individual are constantly interacting with each other, either permitting and encouraging or limiting and discouraging change. As children develop, the constraints change and shape the movement arising from their interaction. This very much fits in with a dynamic model of motor control described later.

Types of change

The result of the change arising from the underlying capacity of the child can be seen, but it is difficult to view change itself. In addition, change is not unidimensional, with varying types of change taking place. A classic paper by Flavell (1972), while not directly addressing motor behaviour, is still helpful today. He describes five types of change that may occur with development.

The first of these is *addition* where a particular behaviour is added to the repertoire and from then on co-exists within the child. Thus, a child who starts to walk adds this to the repertoire of earlier forms of locomotion; the child may not choose to crawl now that s/he can walk but it is still within the repertoire and thus walking is an addition.

A second change is that of *substitution* where one behaviour eventually replaces another. Earlier forms of grasping, using the base of the hand in a clumsy manner, are replaced by a range of grasps including the pincer grip with thumb and finger opposition.

A third type of change is that of *modification* which is used by Flavell to indicate a change in adaptive quality rather than a change of kind, and occurs through generalization, differentiation or stabilization. A good example of this would be a child's modifying their walking pattern to accommodate an uneven or slippery surface such as ice or mud.

Flavell's fourth type of change is *inclusion* and occurs when children incorporate one movement which has integrity on its own into a sequence of movements or becomes part of a higher order movement. An example might be using a finger and thumb opposition into a more complex movement such as rotating a pencil rather than simply holding it, or the use of any simple closed skill such as throwing a ball and changing the environmental context such that there is a moving array and original ball catching is included in a new dynamic context.

Finally, Flavell uses the term *mediation* to indicate that a skill can be a bridge to another skill without actually being part of it. This is a little more difficult in the movement context but one could use manual skills not simply in an instrumental manner to get things done, but also for the child to learn more about his/her environment through the movement. These illustrations are not meant to be definitive in the specific sense that these are the only types of changes that take place. Other categories of change can be presented. However, these are presented as illustrations of the concept that changes are taking place with development, and that change can take a number of different forms.

No matter how change with development is described, the proposal is that the change is interactive or to be more accurate, transactive. This means that the contributing partners to the change process of *person resources, environmental context* and the *task* interact in a dynamic manner such that they themselves are part of the process and the product of change. A park bench is an object to hold on to for a young toddler; for an older child it is something to climb on to; for a teenager it might be to jump over or walk on and for us as we get older it affords sitting down! This dynamic view makes the study more complicated but also makes it much richer in the possibilities it offers not only in the explanation of change but also in what can be done to bring about positive change in those children who have some form of movement difficulty.

The basic line is that there are three components that are influential in the developmental process – the mover, the context and the task – and that each offers a unique opportunity for modification, when presented with a child showing difficulties. This is not simply concentrating on the mover, even though that is the ultimate aim; it is possible to isolate parts of the environment, modify them, present different tasks in a number of different ways in order to facilitate development, which influences the resources of the mover. This in turn changes the mover, who in turn views the context and the task in a different manner, thus changing the dynamics of the movement problem. The next section will explore how these changes take place, examining the different explanations of development but ultimately resting on an explanation that comes within a dynamical systems analysis, which has at its core the three interacting variables we have outlined.

Explanation of change

The most usual activity that we engage in with respect to motor development is to describe the changes that are taking place with its inherent attraction and keen observers performing this with great insight and accuracy. Chapter 2 provides descriptions of the normally expected changes seen in motor development. A more difficult activity is to try and propose explanations for the changes that characterize development. In a number of publications Esther Thelen and her colleagues have made strong arguments for what they term a dynamical systems approach to motor development being a more logical, theoretical and parsimonious explanation to the more usual approaches to explanation (Thelen, 1995; Thelen and Smith, 1994; Ulrich, 1997). The arguments and evidence support this standpoint while recognizing that not all aspects of development have been explored in this manner.

Traditional theories

Traditionally there have been two accepted theories of motor development with the *maturation one* or *neurally based* one being the most widely accepted. Much of this comes from the classic work of some of the early researchers in motor development who observed with great accuracy the developing child and their movements. Most of the work was longitudinal in nature, documenting in detail the sequence of motor development which they attributed to the developing central nervous system (Bayley, 1969a; Gesell, 1928; McGraw, 1932; Shirley, 1931). The changes in the neural system were thought to be programmed over time and the motor development milestones followed this neural unfolding. Ulrich (1997) notes that this is still followed today in some quarters but argues that the maturationist approaches fails to explain behaviour in real time and does not show the process of change. Issues such as how the central nervous system can encode all the material for patterns over a lifespan are not realistically explained with respect to the complexity of movements.

A second explanation that has been proposed for the developmental process is that from *cognitive psychology and information processing*. Fundamentally, this emphasizes plans of behaviour or schemas with researchers such as Piaget (1952) being prominent, followed by research in motor control and learning (see Schmidt and Lee, 1999 for a review). Information processing studies took the motor behaviour field great strides forward with the underlying notion that motor behaviour arises from a series of cognitive acts which begin with the input of information through the sensors, vision and kinaesthesis, and this is transformed on its way through the system of short-term memory, decision making through to motor programmes and the functional act. From these studies we have learned that children, as they increase in age, can move and think faster, are able to employ more sophisticated strategies such as are useful for memory encoding and retrieval and can employ more flexible motor programmes to respond to increasingly complex environmental contexts. However, as Ulrich (1997) points out, information processing models are prescriptive in nature, they do not specify the origin of such constructs as motor programmes, and crucially they virtually ignore the control of movement itself. They give little explanation about how the movement itself is controlled, thus making it difficult to invoke an explanation of how movement develops.

Dynamical systems

The explanation of how movement develops that is favoured here is that of *dynamical systems* which has a number of origins. One strand, derived from mathematics, has been used to explain the development of weather systems, the growth of cities, business and various types of biological systems. In many quarters, it is referred to as complex systems but in the motor development and control arena it is called dynamic systems. Other sources of origin to this come from the work of the Russian physiologist Nicholai Bernstein (1967) and the ecological perception work of J.J. and E.J. Gibson (1979) leading to the motor development work of Thelen. This explanation argues that both neural (maturational) and information processing approaches cannot fully explain the processes of change nor the origins of purposeful goal-directed movements.

Bernstein (1967) rejected the idea that there is a one to one relationship between the precise firing of neurons and the subsequent movement pattern. Actions can be the result of a variety of muscle contraction patterns from different starting points and also the same contractions producing different outcomes, with control emerging as the body interacts with the environment. A key question asks how the independent parts of the body can be organized in order to achieve the action that is intended. These independent variables include limbs, muscles and joints all of which can be configured in a myriad of ways, even to achieve the same goal. Bernstein (1967), recognizing that the same muscle contractions can have different outcomes or conversely different contractions producing the same outcomes all dependent upon context, concluded that actions are planned at an abstract level, and Kugler and Turvey (1987) introduced the term 'softly assembled' to describe the subsystems and components that produce the movement from the available information, allowing for flexibility to meet the specific demands of any task. A hallmark of such systems is the formation of patterns from multiple sources in the environment which are self-organized.

A number of fundamental concepts are involved in the overall theoretical picture of dynamical systems with self-organization being one that is central. In this, motor behaviours are not specified in the brain a priori; there is no central regulator, but actions emerge as the consequence of the cooperation of multiple subsystems and components. The system is open to information flow, leading to a perception–action interaction, and the system becomes self-organizing. These multiple subsystems include intrinsic ones such as neural organization, strength, joints, motivation and emotional state as well as extrinsic ones, such as the nature of the task and the context in which these are situated. The figure from Keogh and Sugden (1985) and Newell's (1986) constraints paper fully fit into this model.

There is strong evidence from some of the locomotion studies by Thelen and her colleagues that motor behaviour in the early years is self-organized and not prescribed. Her work on early walking and stepping, which is elaborated later in the chapter, suggests that subsystems do not supplant the role of the central nervous system, they utilize it, ensuring that it has its role in the overall dynamics with the task and the environment in the developing system. Another principle that is fundamental to the dynamical systems approach is that of context. Examining manual skills, Newell et al. (1989a, b) found that grip patterns emerged as a consequence of the size and structure of the body segments and the task constraints. Similarly, in studies involving reaching and grasping in children with hemiplegic cerebral palsy, it has been shown that children not only move to couple the hands in terms of space and time when performing bimanual reaching, but that changing the context or nature of the task brings about modifications to reaching and grasping on the hemiplegic side. This is in children who by definition have an impaired neural system and by changing the intrinsic and extrinsic constraints of which the neural system plays a part, the reaching and grasping behaviour can be modified (Sugden and Utley, 1995; Utley and Sugden, 1998). These studies showed that different types of coupling did take place in many instances, indicating that intrinsic and extrinsic constraints can affect even constitutionally-based disorders, thus providing an optimistic model for the management of movement disorders through a combination of intrinsic constraints, use of context and the nature of the task.

Using the development of walking as an example, it is clear that it involves much more than maturational processes. It is more of a combination of variables that are currently available in a particular context, and walking becomes self-organized, influenced by a range of intrinsic and extrinsic constraints. Thus, the locomotor changes that take place during the first year of life are influenced by for example, increase in strength, control of head orientation during gaze, unimanual reaching and contralateral leg movements. These and others encourage the emergence of new behaviours which at first are unstable but with experience they become more stable and are generalized across contexts; as one part of the system starts to change again, a shift may occur that again starts a step change in the system with a new motor pattern.

Ecological approach

In order that action can emerge, information needs to enter the system and Gibson and Gibson's ecological approach to perception, also known as direct perception, provides an explanation of this while neatly fitting into a dynamical systems framework (Gibson and Gibson, 1979). To Gibson and Gibson, perception and action are linked with 'affordances' in the environment providing direct possibilities for an individual. The environmental array contains rich available information and affordances are the match between this information and the resources of the child such that actions are produced. In the developing child, affordances are often guided by body-scaled ratios, with an object such as a bench first affords holding on to at shoulder height for a toddler; later climbing on to it in early childhood; and finally sitting on in adulthood. There is no need to relearn any part of the action system or recalculate a movement, the action emerges from the environment-body interaction. An experimental example is provided by van der Kamp et al. (1998) who examined reaching and grasping of different sized cubes in children aged five, seven and nine years. The older children had a higher incidence of one-handed grasps but when the cubes were selected to match the size of the hand, this difference disappeared, indicating that environmental affordances, in this case cube size matching hand size, were perceived by the children and drove the action.

Questions and change

The two issues of description and explanation are highlighted when the development of the young infant from birth to approximately two years of age is examined and described in detail in Chapter 2. Some of the major milestones are described in this period of time, but there are fundamental questions surrounding this development; such as, are the primitive reflexes seen at birth related to the later voluntary skill? How are they related if the answer is yes and how do the reflexes disappear (Goldfield and Wolff, 2004). What other forms of movement activity are present at birth and in the early months and how are they organized with respect to later skill?

Examples are presented to illustrate what changes take place and how they can be accounted for from a dynamical systems perspective. Goldfield and Wolff (2004) view development in a dynamic manner, noting that this type of explanation differs from others in three important ways and link with our description of dynamical systems. First, dynamical systems specify how multiple subcomponents interact to change the system to produce a coordinated whole. They note that sucking, breathing, arm waving and kicking all interact to influence each other. Secondly, it shows how selection processes work with self-organization to produce novel movement patterns. Thus, the perceptual information the infant receives during the act of kicking starts to aid the selection process for a subsequent motor act which itself becomes self-organizing. Following on from this is the third point that the brain and the nervous system are not the sole driver for development but part of a total system working cooperatively. As Goldman and Wolff (2004) note:

> the brain is considered a medium for imposing general laws that yield patterns of coordination, but the brain is not the sole source of coordination and control. (p. 5)

Thus, rather than ascribe to the brain only certain neural properties resulting in limb configurations and thus a maturational explanation of development, it is 'informationally coupled' to a structured environment helping to produce adaptive movements in response to contextual settings (Gibson and Gibson, 1979). Goldman and Wolff (2004) note that the self-organizational quality is evident in babies when rhythmical behaviours such as breathing and sucking influence each other and become coupled together in a new way. In effect, the self-organizing behaviours of sucking and breathing start to influence each other into a new self-organizing pattern. It is the parsimonious explanation of the origins of some motor acts from a dynamical systems viewpoint that makes it so attractive.

One question that is often asked is how an infant moves from a stable pattern of motor behaviour to another one. As Goldman and Wolff (2004) point out, the infant locomotion studies of Gesell (1946) and McGraw (1963) describe the stage like progression from creeping to crawling with different motor patterns in each. However, not all infants progress in this way with some going directly to crawling while others crawl before they creep. A similar range of progressions is observed in reaching and grasping, showing that there are multiple pathways to the end goal. Earlier, the work of Thelen has been described and how it has influenced our thinking concerning the development of locomotion by examining the influence of constraints that are not neural, such as the biomechanical properties of limbs, their morphology and the elastic properties of muscles and how these affect the change in walking patterns from the early stereotypic leg flexions and extensions to the complex and varied patterns required for adaptive walking. The information came from studies in infants before they could walk and this transition took place in leg kicking movements between the ages of three and seven months because of the changing properties of the limbs, not because of neural development. This is presented to show that changes from a stable state to one that is more functionally adaptive involve multiple subsystems that organize themselves with the brain and neural system not being totally responsible for this change but being part of the overall system with a functional controlling role.

The concept of 'attractor' is one that is used in dynamic systems and it is employed to describe preferred patterns of behaviour such that the child or the system wishes to perform. An attractor has a stability to it that is the result of previous history, the child's resources, the goal and the task set in context. Attractors change because of the complex interactions between the various subcomponents which cause the system to become unstable until a new alternative is established. This progression is seen in locomotion whereby rolling is replaced by crawling due to changes in the underlying constraints or variables eventually leading to the walking attractor being the one that is most stable. In the early transition from one attractor to another the system is variable and unstable; for example, in the early stages of walking an infant may revert to crawling because it gives a more immediate advantage because of the instability of the new attractor walking. However, as walking becomes more established through experience, crawling almost disappears as a form of locomotion and will only be used under instruction or in specific types of context.

It is not the function of this text to explore in detail the intricacies of all dynamic systems and the fundamental questions that are being examined. It is simply sufficient to note these and to argue that they represent a considerable step forward in the understanding of motor development. The logical step from this is to show how this kind of theorizing leads to better and more appropriate types of intervention such that we base our methods on evidence, particularly with respect to the different constraints that can help and guide or perversely hinder attempts at remediation.

The study of change

There is here a preference for a dynamic systems approach to explanations of motor development, but whatever explanation is presented, the concept of change is central to all of them. The question becomes how change is recognized, and to answer this there are a number of ways in which studies are designed.

Ideally, a group of children is followed for a given period of time, which could be days or weeks or even years, and plot the change in the variable that is being measured. This is known as *longitudinal research* and while it would seem to be an ideal way of collecting data, it is not only expensive but because of the intensity of the study in some studies that last years, not many can be completed in a researcher's career. Some form of compromise is usually taken. For example, when change is rapid as in early childhood, the intensity of the observation is high; however, as the child develops, changes occur more slowly, and the observation regimes are not nearly as intense.

A more parsimonious method of collecting developmental data is from what is called *cross-sectional* studies. In these studies, data is collected at one period in time, but it is collected on several age groups simultaneously. For example, if it is wished to determine what the course reaction time takes with age, groups of children aged 6, 8, 10 and 12 years would be tested, giving developmental progressions from aged 6 to 12. It is data that is relatively easy to collect, and can be done in a short period of time. However, using this method, true developmental change data is not being collected; it is being inferred from the different age groups that, hopefully, are comparable through the procedures.

In order to try and minimize the disadvantages of both cross-sectional and longitudinal methods while at the same time optimizing their advantages, researchers have used combinations. For example, it is possible to accelerate longitudinal methods by involving children at aged 4, 6, 8 and 10 years of age, and if the children were studied for a period of two years, data would be available on children from four to 14 years of age. In addition, because of the two-year length of study, checks can be made on the original six year olds at the end of the study when the original four year olds were six; similarly this could be done with all of the other ages apart from the original four year olds. Thus, in a two year time period it has been possible to examine an age span of 10 years with checks to ensure that the original cohorts of children are comparable samples and are not significantly different from each other.

Motor control and learning

A final comment on motor development is to note the massive contribution made by the research in motor control and learning. This is usually concerned with adult performance but many of the same principles apply to the developmental scene. *Motor control* refers to the manner in which the central nervous system is organized so that the many limbs, joints and muscles are organized and coordinated to produce smooth skilful bodily movement. In addition, the study of motor control and performance is taken at one snapshot in time; when a person throws or catches a ball, the study of the processes involved in this is motor control or performance. This is contrasted with *motor learning* which is the study of how individual movements are performed differently as a result of practice or experience. In many definitions or descriptions of motor learning, four distinct characteristics are usually included (Schmidt and Lee, 1999). First, learning is a process and involves a set of underlying events or changes that occur when people practise and this enables them to become more skilled. Secondly, learning is the direct result of practice or experience. Thirdly, learning cannot actually be directly observed; it is only the results of learning that can be observed and measured as the underlying processes are internal and are not accessible. Thus learning has to be observed from a change in performance. Finally, learning is relatively permanent; that is it is not a one shot performance that could be the result of a temporary variable such as fatigue or motivation that could be easily reversed. Bringing these four together, Schmidt and Lee (1999) define motor learning as

> a set of processes associated with practice or experience leading to relatively permanent changes in the capability for movement. (p. 264)

It is easy to see how many of these processes overlap with development and they become particularly important when children with motor coordination difficulties are considered, and approaches to intervention are examined (Chapter 5).

CHAPTER 2

Motor development in young children

Introduction

Watching young children develop skills that allow them to move around the environment or manipulate objects is a constant source of interest and fascination to us. Adults, often as parents, chronicle the milestones of babies and young children, and after two years realize how fast these changes have taken place. At birth, a baby is dependent on an older person for even a change of position, yet by the end of the second year of life, the young infant can move in a variety of ways, in a number of contexts and use their hands to manipulate a wide range of objects. In many of these movements they are still immature, but the change is astonishing and it is a safe statement to make that they never make such progress again throughout their lives. Although babies at birth are dependent on more competent others, they do have a number of core movements, some of them reflexive, others more voluntary and these rudimentary movements are the foundation and building blocks for the fundamental movement skills that we see developing during the first six or seven years of life.

By this age, most young children will have developed these fundamental movement skills, and although after this, children go on to use these skills in a variety of ways, play with them, become more proficient and increase in performance, they do not develop totally new skills. It is difficult to identify naturally developing movement skills that emerge after this age. New specific sports skills are learned, such as skateboarding but by six or seven years of age the fundamental skills are all in place with the child being able to run, jump, hop, skip, climb, throw, catch, strike, wash, dress, write and draw, all with some degree of competence. With this in mind, it is essential that all children have the opportunity for the development of these skills in the early years such that they can be later used in sporting, recreational, classroom, social and home situations.

This chapter describes the development of movement skills during these first six or seven years. The first two years of life are described followed by a summary of the years two/three to six/seven. This text is concerned with the condition of Developmental Coordination Disorder (DCD), yet nearly all of the literature on children with DCD has concentrated on the primary school years, five to eleven, and consequently our knowledge of the early years is fairly scanty. However, the years up to six or seven are crucial for the development of those important fundamental motor skills, without which the everyday skills that allow a child to interact, with peers, play sports, write and draw with fluency, be involved in different forms of recreation and generally be competent in the motoric demands of everyday life would be seriously lacking. It is also known that although most children who enter school at around five years of age arrive with a range of skills that allow them to successfully negotiate the movement problems that are present in their everyday life, there are a few children whose lack of skills are a cause for concern for parents, teachers or themselves. In Chapter 3 these children are described together with the consequences of this lack of skill, but in order to place them in perspective, this chapter describes the normally developing child acquiring movement skills during the early years.

Motor development from birth to two years of age

Early movements

During the first two years of life babies begin to gain control over their own movements. At birth, they are dependent on others to change from any position in which they are placed but by 24 months of age there is a general expectation that they can make many postural adjustments, walk and can handle many objects. Early movement development involves basic postural control leading to locomotion and providing the stability for manual control.

Movements of newborn babies will involve those that are *reflexive* in nature and those that seem to be more random in nature called *spontaneous movements*. Information on reflexes has been available for some considerable time but it is only in the last twenty years or so that those apparently random movements have been examined in more detail being reclassified as spontaneous movements, so called because they apparently appear without stimulation. In the following sections both reflexes and spontaneous movements are examined without providing a comprehensive review but with explanations about their origins and how they relate to the later motor behaviour with which we are more familiar.

Reflexes

Reflexes are most simply described as involuntary movements, often stereotypical, in response to a given stimulus which can be light or sound, touch or pressure on the body or its parts. Reflexes are expected at particular ages, some disappearing soon afterwards, others staying longer and remain throughout life, while others appear to be the basis of voluntary control. Tests of reflexes such as the APGAR scale (1953) are often given to babies at birth to ensure that they are of the expected intensity, complete and showing symmetry.

Many primitive reflexes are present at or before birth. For example, sucking, which appears before birth and continues throughout life, although the mechanism changes as it develops into voluntary control rather than being an involuntary reflex to a given stimulus such as a bottle or a nipple. The rooting reflex is one that serves a purpose for a short period of time and then disappears when a larger range of movements appear making responses more adaptable. The reflex is elicited when there is pressure on the cheek which results in the head and in particular the mouth moving towards this pressure, serving to locate a breast or bottle. After three or four months following birth, the baby has other means of locating milk and this reflex disappears. A point made later is that many early reflexes disappear or are subsumed under voluntary control for more adaptive movements to develop. Sucking is something that continues throughout life but comes under voluntary control while rooting appears for a short while and then disappears. The palmar grasp is a reflex that is familiar to many of us. If a finger is placed across the palm, infant and babies will flex their fingers to close around the finger or object with quite a tight grip. Parents show off their babies by lifting them up in this situation. This reflex continues through the first five or six months of life and then disappears again to be replaced by a more voluntary control of grasping. This voluntary control involves opening the hand and fingers prior to touching the object, in other words anticipating a grip and this anticipation with development becomes more refined with respect to the physical properties of the object as determined by vision. Reflexes are also used as indicators that the system is not developing in an appropriate manner, either by the non and late appearance of a reflex, or through the continuation of one long after it should have disappeared. This can happen because of some impairment from birth or after some form of brain injury. In the latter case, if the injury is healed, the reflexes often disappear suggesting that higher neural centres do suppress the reflex in preparation for more adaptive voluntary movements. A short list of early reflexes, their appearance and disappearance is presented in Table 2.1.

The walking reflex is one that epitomizes some of the debate in how and why children develop motor skills. Parents, siblings or friends have

Table 2.1 Selected reflexes in young infants

Reflex	Stimulus	Description	Appearance	Disappearance
Sucking	Touching lips	Sucking motion	Prenatal	3–4 months
Palmar grasp	Touch palm	Flexion on object	Prenatal	4–6 months
Asymmetrical tonic neck	Turn head to one side	Same-side arm and leg extend	Prenatal	4–6 months
Babinski	Stroke sole	Toes extend	Birth	4 months
Walking	Hold upright and place infant on flat surface	Walking pattern in legs	Birth	4–5 months

Source: Keogh and Sugden (1985, p. 26)

seen babies held under the arms and their feet allowed to touch a flat surface. This is immediately followed by an effort by the baby at what looks like a walking action. This appears at birth and seemingly disappears at around five months of age.

The case of the 'disappearing reflex' raises an important issue that permeates through the whole motor development literature. The issue concerns what the relationship is between a given reflex and a similar voluntary movement that appears later. There are only really two possible answers to this and the first which is favoured by maturationists such as McGraw (1963) would argue that the two are not related and are separate. In McGraw's view, the reflexive stepping would actually interfere with voluntary movement and so must be inhibited before voluntary walking can come in.

However, from a dynamical systems analysis of motor development there is an interesting alternative. Some of the principles upon which a dynamical systems explanation are based include multiple subsystems contributing to the developmental process with the nervous system being just one of these subsystems; that the behaviour is self-organized with no central executor as the maturationists would ascribe to the brain, and that the changes are abrupt or non-linear in nature. When these principles are taken together with some of the work by Esther Thelen, her colleagues and others, there are some rather interesting results. One of the first studies was by Zelazo et al. (1972a, b) who gave daily practice in the walking reflex to a group of infants and showed that this actually increased the stepping reflex and also resulted in the earlier onset of voluntary walking compared to a non-practising group. They suggested that the reason for the disappearance of the reflex was lack of use and inhibition of the reflex as suggested by maturationists was not necessary for voluntary stepping.

In the early 1980s Thelen and her colleagues began a series of classic studies which took this notion further with some quite startling conclusions. Here, only a short summary of some of the work is presented while recognizing that these experiments have had considerable impact on the way infant development is viewed.

Thelen and her colleagues analysed the role of factors other than neural linkages for the changes in the precursors to walking with, for example, both biomechanical and morphological variables being found to have an impact. One such finding was that the kicking movements of infants while lying on their backs appeared to have the same movement patterns as later stepping. Kicking appears early in life and, unlike stepping, does not disappear after a few months. When a kinematic analysis was performed on both kicking and stepping, no noticeable differences were found, leading Thelen (1995) to conclude that they were the same movements preformed in different postures and that it is hardly likely that the neural system would work to inhibit one of these movements and not the other as would be suggested by a maturationist viewpoint. Thelen and Fisher (1982, 1983) noticed that at just around the same time as stepping disappears, infants are gaining weight, most of it due to subcutaneous fat rather than muscle mass, and they concluded that the disappearance of the stepping action was not so much due to neural inhibition but a combination of a biomechanically and heavier but not stronger limbs. In later investigations, the stepping reflex was found to be either facilitated, by immersing in water, or inhibited by the addition of weights. Thelen (1995) is not claiming that simply biomechanical factors are responsible for development but more that it can be shown to be one factor in the multicausal subcomponents that need to be taken into consideration, and it is not simply a question of the brain dictating events through maturational processes.

In another series of studies, Thelen and Ulrich (1991) placed infants as young as one month old on a treadmill and found that if they were supported under the arms, they could perform coordinated alternative stepping movements which shared many kinematic patters of adult walking. The development of stepping does not reside in the baby or in the treadmill, as Thelen (1995) notes:

all behaviour is always an emergent property of a confluence of factors. (p. 83)

Thelen also conducted investigations that pointed towards the view that motor behaviour is self-organized. Infants who were supported under the arms were placed on a treadmill responded immediately to the dynamics of the context by showing alternating steps. These were infants who were not yet pulling to standing but across a range of treadmill speeds their responses remained stable (Thelen, 1986). Even when the treadmill was split with one half moving at a different speed to the other, an immediate shift in the leg-cycle duration occurred, so maintaining the alternation of the legs. This could be compared to a four-legged animal such as a horse which changes from walking to trotting to cantering to galloping all immediately and self-organized.

The explanation of the relationship of reflexes to voluntary control fits neatly into a dynamical systems approach to motor development. This type of information and approach is also applicable to children as they develop from three to six or seven years of age, in that influences on development are multiple, interact with each other, are non-linear and self-organizing, all characteristics of a dynamic system.

Spontaneous movements

One of the other characteristics of young babies is the seemingly random movements which appear to have no purpose. It was long thought that these movements were not organized and served very little purpose in contrast to reflexes which, as noted, have very definite purposes. These movements involved squirming bodies, waving arms and legs, stretching fingers and toes and appear not to have any relationship to future movements. However, with work again from Thelen, these assumptions appear to be incorrect and indeed the movements do seem to contain much more in terms of intention and organization that had been previously thought (Thelen, 1985; 1995; Thelen and Fisher, 1983; Thelen et al., 1983).

In one of these movements, that of supine kicking, the movement is not random and there is a specific organization to it with the hip, knee and ankle all working in tandem with each other to produce what we would call a coordinated action. The kicking involved those subcomponents of flexion–pause–extension between kick interval, similar to adult stepping. They are not the same as adult stepping, being more variable and joints are moved in unison rather than in sequence. However, they are not random, nor are they reflexes which respond to specific stimuli but are spontaneous movements that do develop over the first six months to produce a coordinated pattern. In addition, these spontaneous movements are obvious precursors to the voluntary controlled, goal directed actions we see later in early infancy.

Description of change

In Chapter 1, an explanation of how children change is offered using a dynamical systems approach. In this chapter, descriptions of change are outlined, though it is not the intention to describe all of the developments that take place from birth to two years of age but simply summarize the types of landmark achievements that can be expected during this period.

Examples of these would include standing upright, walking and reaching and grasping, and although ages in weeks can be given for each of these activities and their subcomponents, age should be taken as approximate and only indicative of normative achievement, with variability an expectation. In addition, they are not to be taken as invariant sequences but only as patterns of change as although the general patterns are similar there are often different ways of achieving them. A simple example is that crawling and creeping precedes walking in most children but in some, crawling, as we know it, does not appear and children move around in other ways such as 'bottom shuffling' before achieving upright locomotion. Another consideration when examining infants' motoric progress is that movement is often used as an indicator of other aspects of development, such as socialization, with the result that movement behaviours selected for observations are insufficient to describe in detail movement development.

There are infant scales which comprehensively chronicle the movement behaviours of young infants; two have been drawn up in order to provide a comprehensive picture. The result in Figures 2.1, 2.2, and 2.3a, b and c are taken from a compilation from Keogh and Sugden (1985) based on original data from the Bayley Scales of Infant Development (Bayley, 1969b) and the Denver Developmental Screening Test (Frankenburg and Dodds, 1967) and represent the development of postural control, locomotion and manual control respectively. The two scales are scored slightly differently with both providing a median age of achievement (50th percentile), but differ in other aspects. Each activity is represented by a 'box' or rectangular frame, the outline of which represents the variability on that particular activity. For the Bayley, the left-hand side of the box indicates the age at which 5 per cent of children achieve the activity, with the right-hand side indicating achievement of 95 per cent of the children. For the Denver, the corresponding figures are 25 per cent and 90 per cent. In some cases the items are not totally similar, and in others the activity only appears on one scale but the overall picture is not distorted and similar profiles are presented. As is always the case with scales, they should be treated with caution, recognizing they are the result of group data, and are only general indicators of change.

Postural control

Postural control and locomotion are linked; babies need to control their posture so they can gain control over their other movements. For example, there is a whole series of postural control actions that need to be achieved before a baby can stand which is the precursor to the locomotor activity of walking. Postural control from this perspective is part of all movements by underlying them. One has only to be in a clinical situation to see the difference in the reaching and grasping of a child with cerebral palsy when the trunk is stabilized by the child or through some form of assistance, from a situation where there is no stabilization and the reaching and grasping action is disrupted.

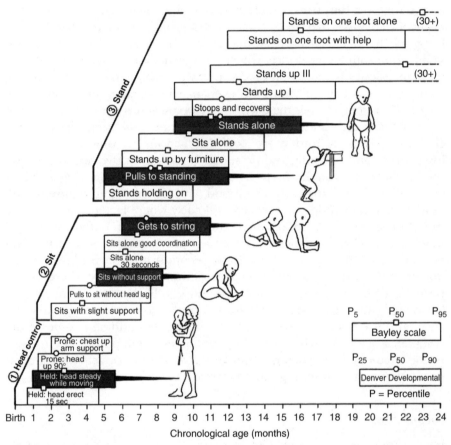

Figure 2.1 Development of postural control. Source: Keogh and Sugden (1985, p. 32).

In Figure 2.2 there is a description of the development of postural control during the first couple of years after birth. In the early months, there is the beginning of head control with the lifting of the head also involving extending the arms, noting that head control is basic to all other forms of postural control. The next stage is the development of upright posture, moving from a situation at around three months when babies can sit with support to around five months when they can sit without support. Again, this unsupported sitting is another major landmark in babies' development. From there, a baby progresses to a situation where they move themselves to a sitting position from a prone or supine position, and at this stage can also roll from back to front and vice versa. The movement to sitting now allows babies to do other things such as turn and look at objects and have a greater range of reaching and grasping. The third important progression in the development of postural control is to move to an upright position and by around seven to eight months babies can pull themselves to stand which coincides with their being able to roll over, thus considerably increasing their movement repertoire. The result of all of this is that babies can now change their position rather than just being able to hold it. Finally, at around 11 months of age the babies are able to stand alone without assistance, which is a precursor to walking. In between these milestones is the action of sitting down which is not, as often noted, identical to standing up! Again this overlaps with standing up, showing the increased movement skills the child is developing at this age.

After these early ages, postural control is not something often chronicled as it is built into more complex actions of different types of locomotion and reaching and grasping. However, in two areas it is indirectly followed through, the first being in the various balancing activities engaged in from later early childhood. The second is in children with more severe difficulties such as cerebral palsy where lack of postural control of various types is often a distinguishing feature. In both of these, the fundamental characteristics of postural control emerge: first, it involves the child maintaining a steady position, secondly involves the child changing position and achieving a new position; and thirdly, there is the problem of how to maintain balance and equilibrium while moving. In balancing activities these are globally referred to as static and dynamic balance, and are necessary when we are in different and sometimes more complex situations such as standing on one leg while putting on trousers (static balance), or engaging in fundamental locomotor activities such as running, jumping, hopping etc. (dynamic balance).

Locomotion

During the first two months after birth, babies are generally not mobile; they remain in the position they are placed. During the first year of life they progress from this to being able to move across the ground in a horizontal position and later to walk in an upright stance. Figure 2.2 illustrates this progression.

In the early months babies do move their arms and legs which can move their bodies a little along the ground or to change direction and later to roll over. Early on, babies do bring their knees up under the body by flexing them, followed by extension giving change in direction but often remain in prone position. In the supine position, babies can give a wider range of arm and leg movements, because of the lack of any supporting constraints, but they need to be in a prone position in order to engage in effective change of location.

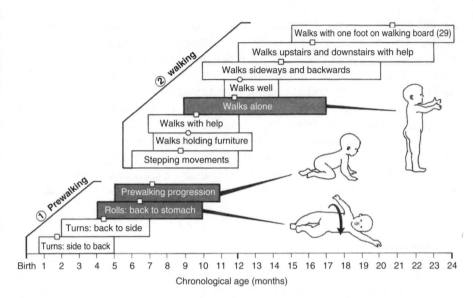

Figure 2.2 Development of locomotion. Source: Keogh and Sugden (1985, p. 38).

During the second six months of life, babies do start to change positions, usually beginning with rolling over from supine to prone position and vice versa, and can result in substantial change in position by successive rolls. By around seven months babies start to move forward in the prone position by crawling or creeping. The former is distinguished by involving the tummy and chest on the ground and the use of either arms or legs or both, while the latter creeping is when the child is on all fours with palms and knees to toes being the contact point and movement is either through homolateral movements, legs and arms on the same side going back and forth together, or contralateral movements when the left arm moves in time with the right leg and vice versa. Numerous variations are evident in these actions and, as has been previously mentioned, many babies do not creep or crawl but find other means by which to change positions.

In addition, one must not think that just because a baby does not creep there is something wrong and it is indicative of impaired development in functions such as visual, cognitive or further motor skills. This was a prevalent view 30 or 40 years ago but current research suggests that infants develop normally even if they do not creep or crawl before they walk (Haywood and Getchell, 2001). However, there are ongoing investigations looking retrospectively at children who are later diagnosed as having DCD. Preliminary reports suggest that there is a higher incidence of non-creepers and non-crawlers in a DCD group than in matched non-DCD peers (Kirby-personal correspondence).

One of the great landmarks in any baby's life is the first unaided step and the development of walking. Around 12 months of age is a time when a child achieves this milestone. As can be seen from Figure 2.2, there is variation with early walkers showing unaided stepping at nine months with others being as late as 17 months. As soon as babies develop this skill, they start to modify it in different ways, by walking sideways and backwards, stopping and changing directions, and by doing other things while they are walking. From these simplest forms, these modifications are repeated through life to more complex walking skills and locomotor activities. The progression from the first few uneasy steps has been chronicled in great detail by some of the early researchers/clinicians such as Shirley (1931). These are fascinating accounts of individual styles in early walking ranging from Harvey who stamped as he walked through Martin the infant Hercules to the twins 'Winnie walker' and 'Fred talker'!

Manual control

Manual control is the general term for the movements of the hands and the arm used to control objects. The hand is used to grasp objects either by the palm or fingers or both and also to manipulate an object when it is in the hand. The arm is used to support the hand in a number of its functions, to position it, as a force when used in conjunction with the hand. Although it is clear that the hands and arms can be separated for analysis like this, it is also clear that they work most of the time as a hand–arm linkage. For example, when using scissors, the arm positions the hand in a particular place, supports the hand as the fingers are used for the scissoring action. Also in the simple action of picking a coin out of a pocket and placing it in a shopkeeper's hand involves positioning the hand supporting it, while the hand is engaged in a number of manipulative activities. The arm is also used to generate force as in pounding with a hammer while the hand is simply grasping the hammer. The hand is a very subtle part of the body with a myriad of uses and a distinguished body of literature describing its uses, history and place in human life (Wilson, 1998; Wing et al., 1996). The hand's first function is that of gripping with varicous types of grips being available to us – such as power or precision grip. In both of these the object remains stable in the hand. The second type of function is manipulation in which the fingers and thumb are used in unison to change the position of an object. Although it is rarely used in this context, manipulation is often involved when releasing an object such as throwing a ball, and it is specifically employed when imparting spin on a ball such as in bowling in cricket. The development of early manual control is shown in Figure 2.3 a, b and c.

The three figures illustrate three parts of manual skills: one (Figure 2.3a) showing hand control and the ability to grasp, hold, handle and release an object; the second (Figure 2.3b) illustrates changes in the arm linkage

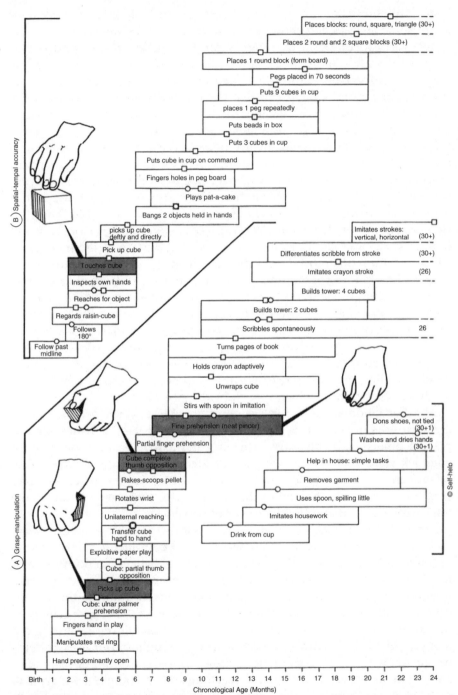

Figure 2.3a, b and c Development of manual control. Source: Keogh and Sugden (1985, p. 46).

system to achieve greater spatial accuracy; the third (Figure 2.3c) is more of a functional analysis and shows the achievement of self-help skills.

Just as in locomotion there are some landmarks which stand out in every baby's life (Figure 2.3a). For example, a significant achievement is reaching and grasping an object such as a cube which occurs around three to four months of age. At first the grasp is primitive with the baby not using the thumb but engaging the heel of the palm and holding it in by the fingers. At five to six months, the thumb is brought into play against the fingers with little or no involvement of the palm. As the child progresses, at around nine or ten months, they begin to pick up smaller objects and the thumb and index finger become opposed forming a pincer grip. This is an important landmark as it shows a precision grip has been achieved and digital control of an object is then possible. The classic film analysis of Halverson (1931) has been extended by Connolly and Elliott (1972) and shows in babies how they progress in the manner in which the thumb is moved, and the placement of an object in the hand. Early in life, before six months of age, infants have only pseudo opposition of the thumb and index finger, that is the thumb comes alongside the finger and does not oppose the finger tip. By eight months of age this pseudo opposition becomes true opposition. In a similar vein, when an object such as a cube is grasped, the action shifts from a palmar to a digital grip which is to a more distal and radial location of the object in the hand, enabling the neat pincer grasp and general precision grip leading to the added dexterity which is seen by the first birthday.

Another landmark is the releasing of an object which occurs around eight months of age and is a precursor to a number of activities such as placing objects and releasing them in a particular location, or in more complex skills such as throwing a ball. By the end of the first year, the infant can stir with a spoon, hold a crayon in a position to scribble and turn book pages. By the end of the second year, they can scribble, make lines with a crayon and build a tower of six blocks.

Figure 2.3b illustrates how vision is employed to achieve greater accuracy of the hand, often referred to as eye-hand coordination. Progression in this area is very swift and by six months of age babies can position their hands accurately and easily. By 12 months they can place their finger in a hole on a pegboard and put three cubes in a cup, and during the second year they can place different shaped objects through the appropriate hole in a form board. Reaching and grasping is a skill that develops during the first year of life and is one that stays with us throughout our lives; it helps us interact with our environment; it allows us to control our environment and is a major survival skill. At first, reaching and grasping is a unitary skill with babies reaching with their entire bodies so that trunk and both hands move towards the object. Later at around four to five months of age, they differentiate into the two separate and recombinable components of reaching and grasping, and at this age they become quite accurate, rarely missing an object when only a couple of months earlier the 'hit rate' can be as low as 40 per cent.

Figure 2.3c shows that few self-help and functional skills are observed in the first year except for a crude use of a spoon and feeding a cracker. The achievement of a pincer grip allowing precision is a major move forward which will later help them in skills such as dressing and feeding. Bimanual skills often come into play in self-help skills, particularly at ages two to seven years, but in the first year it is more often seen in play situations such as transferring blocks from hand to hand and holding a block with one hand for exploration by the other hand (five to six months). In the second year of life, self-help skills are starting to be seen such as attempts to put on shoes or washing and drying hands. Bimanual coordination of the hands is complex as it can involve asymmetrical activities such as the block transference noted above where each hand performs a different task, or symmetrical activities such as the very early one of banging two cubes together which simultaneously moves the two hands towards each other or in playing pat-a-cake. It is interesting to note that symmetrical bimanual movements follow on from the asymmetrical ones.

During the first two years of life, the emphasis is on gaining control of basic self-movements. During the first few months after birth these are characterized by either reflexes or spontaneous movements, both of which we now believe are fundamental to the development of voluntary movement. By two years of age, the infant has a good repertoire of movements involving posture, locomotion and manual dexterity, and they are becoming more continuous than discrete, and definite coordinated movements are clearly present. Major landmarks such as walking occur roughly at one year of age and then during the second year, refinement takes place through steps becoming more continuous and less widely spaced, a lowering of the arms and moving in time with the opposite leg, and an increase and speed with change of direction, often showing different walks. However, at two years of age babies still have a long way to go to achieve anything like mature patterns in locomotion and manual skills, and difficulties are encountered when walking too fast with the child finding control a problem. In addition, if the environment starts to change, that is move or is variable, the two-year-old child will have difficulty in adapting to this change.

One can summarize crudely the development in the first two years of life by dividing the time period into six monthly intervals (Keogh and Sugden, 1985). In the first six months the infant is gaining control of posture to sit without support; locomotion is limited to rolling over or spinning; and manual grasping becomes voluntary but undifferentiated. During the next six months the infant gains more control of posture, enabling locomotion through creeping or crawling and alternatives, can stand and start upright locomotion; they differentiate their grasp and use thumb and index finger in true opposition. From 12 to 18 months, upright mobility is achieved together with the initial use of utensils and during the final six months, there is faster, more reliable, controlled and variable mobility together with some initial achievement of self-help skills.

Motor development from two to seven years of age

The period from two to seven years of age is again one of great change with children at the end of this period being able to have good body control enabling them to participate in many play game situations as well as being competent in many functional manual skills. They will be able to run, jump, hop, skip, climb, catch, kick, strike, write, draw, manipulate *to a certain degree*. These are the fundamental motor skills which are necessary for engaging in functional, self-help and recreational everyday activities, and a normally developing child will be competent to a degree in these. They are also necessary as the building blocks for the more varied and complex motor skills that appear later through sporting activities, classroom demands and social interactions. Earlier the statement was made that we believe that this age range is so important because this is the time these fundamental skills are laid down and there are few if any that naturally emerge after this age. Thus, appropriate exposure to a wide range of these activities is crucial during these years. At the end of this period, they will still continue to find open movement situations demanding, those that involve responding to a moving environment or a moving other person. In addition, after this period, children continue to develop by increasing their level of performance and variety of movement skills in order to cope with their more demanding movement environments whether at home, at school or in other situations.

Body control

In the previous section, activities were divided into those of posture, locomotion and manual skills. However, it was noted that progress in posture becomes difficult to chronicle as it becomes subsumed under other activities. For this reason, the recommendation of Keogh and Sugden (1985) is accepted that locomotion and posture become subsumed under the generic heading of body control, while recognizing that other activities such as throwing will come into play. This section examines the development of body control following the progression in the six areas of walking running, jumping, throwing, hopping and balancing, noted by Keogh and Sugden (1985).

Table 2.2 Body control framework and percentage passing at age 5

Position		Task		Boys	Girls
In place	Hold	Heel-Toe Stand	(R)	78	83
			(L)	83	87
		One-Leg Stand	(R)	61	67
			(L)	52	70
	Controlled	Heel-Toe Touch	(R)	57	72
			(L)	50	61
		Ring-over-Foot	(R)	54	70
			(L)	76	76
	Explosive	Jump-Turn			
		Backward		80	80
		90°		85	91
		180°		50	57
		Hop-Turn			
		Forward		78	78
		Backward		13	46
		90°		53	52
Travelling		Heel-Toe Walk			
		Forward		65	87
		Backward		7	15
		Total mean score (standard deviation)			
		Age 5		16.2 (5.6)	18.6 (6.4)
		Age 6		21.9 (4.5)	24.8 (4.7)
		Age 7		26.0 (3.1)	27.8 (3.5)

Source: Keogh and Sugden (1985, p. 73)

Walking

There is a continuation in the refinement of walking that was evident in the first two years with the legs and arms alternating and the legs being placed in a narrower stance which is less stable but more efficient for walking. Walking becomes more efficient in two important ways. First, it can be varied to include tiptoe walking or walking backwards and can be done in different environmental circumstances such as walking up-hill and down-hill, on uneven or slippery surfaces. It also can be done at faster or slower pace and in step with another person. Secondly, walking becomes much more automatic, leaving the child to be able to perform another task at the same time. So a child can walk and talk at the same time or manipulate an object while walking. Stair climbing is an example of how children are required to adjust their walking to environmental demands and eventually use alternating steps. Children can go upstairs with alternating steps sooner than they can go downstairs – often by as much as 15 months. For example Keogh and Sugden (1985) report that stair climbing with 'marking time' steps occurs between 24 and 28 months while descent is between 28 and 34 months. Using alternating steps, climbing occurs between 31 and 41 months while descending is between 49 and 55 months. Stair climbing and particularly stair descending illustrates how the environment is a constraint constantly making demands on the child, and as the child progresses through these early years, these demands are all met with competence.

Running

The obvious difference between running and walking is that in running the mover is airborne at some time during the cycle. At 18 months children begin running, by 24 months most can run. By four to six years of age children have a good running form and start to use running in play-game situations. The components in the action of running occur so quickly that it is difficult to observe for comments. However, by the naked eye it is possible to focus on one part of the skill such as arm action and observe that; alternatively video is quick and easy to use for observation purposes, with the general tip that it is advantageous to watch from the side to trace leg movements, and from the rear to examine elbows and heels. Early running is characterized by the legs having a limited range of motion; and arms and thighs being slightly to the side, rather than directly forward and back. It is probably not coordination that limits running in the first stages as walking had been established for some time with similar movement patterns. Running involves both feet being off the ground at the same time and strength is needed for this and it is a strong candidate for being a rate limiter (Clark and Whitall, 1989). Another rate limiter is balance; a child has to maintain this as s/he must maintain control as s/he lands after being in the air. With development, the proficient runner increases stride length, reduces and eliminates lateral arm and leg movements to adopt a heel-toe landing and the trunk leans slightly forward in preparation for this.

Jumping

A jump is usually a single discrete movement which takes the body off the ground and can involve either a one- or two-foot take-off and a one- or two-foot landing. It becomes more complex when one takes off one foot and lands on the same foot as this is a hop, and taking off one foot and landing on the other is a stride or long step. Age of achievement of various types of jump varies but the general pattern is consistent. Stepping down from a step occurs around 18 months of age, and this one-foot take-off precedes a two-foot take-off. An important milestone is the two-foot jump from the ground which can start in a rudimentary fashion at around the second birthday which in the first instance is usually up and down rather than forward. A standing long jump is the one that is usually chronicled and this involves a two-footed take-off to a two-foot landing as shown in Figure 2.4.

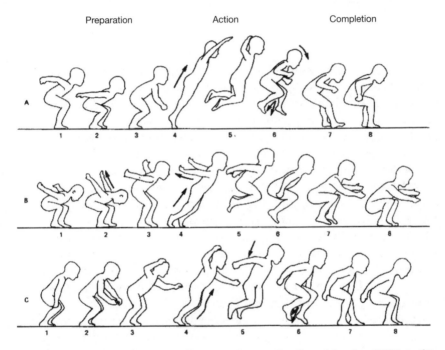

Figure 2.4 Movement mechanisms in jumping. Source: Keogh and Sugden (1985, p. 63).

The task here was to jump as far as possible but it is the manner in which it is accomplished that is interesting. Child A has adequate form to summon the forces necessary for the jump but the head goes down in mid-flight, the arms and legs are not completely symmetrical and the legs are extended too soon in preparation for landing. Child B is a mixture of movement characteristic of younger children. There is an extreme crouch at the beginning, with arms held way back. At take-off, the leg and trunk extensions are well coordinated and forward but the arms, instead of moving forward, remain behind the body. Symmetry is good but the lack of appropriate arm action is a limiting factor. Child C shows an incomplete jump with not enough force. The legs are not fully extended on take-off and the trunk is drawn up and back rather than forward. Arms rotate up and back and the legs are flexed for landing soon after take-off.

Distances for jumping are also good indicators of developmental progression and expectancies are that for a standing long jump the following would be average expectancies: 20 inches at three; 27 inches at four; 38 inches at five; 43 inches at six. Haywood and Getchell (2001) usefully present types of jumps arranged by progressive difficulty, ranging from jumping down from one foot, down from two to two through running and jumping from one foot to two feet and jumping from two feet to two feet over an object.

Hopping

Hopping is used in many playground games and involves a series of discrete movements which are difficult to make continuously because the same leg is involved on take-off and landing, thus making demands on coordination and strength. The better the hopping is controlled, the easier it is to make continuous movements and alterations. Achievements in hopping have been chronicled numerous times and can be summarized by the following: by around 40 months children can hop once and by 60 months can perform 10 hops. There are gender difference in these achievements with hopping five times on one foot being achieved by 67 per cent of boys at 66 months and 90 per cent of girls at the same age (Keogh, 1968). Early hopping is characterized by a low hop with the other leg flexed and not working with the arms. With development, the non-hopping leg becomes the swing leg, leading the hop with the opposite arm moving forward at the same time. Details of the various stages can be found in Haywood and Getchell (2001).

Hopping soon becomes part of other locomotor activities such as skipping and galloping. Skipping, which is a step hop followed by another step hop on the opposite side, starts at around 43 months on one foot and on alternate feet at around 60 months. Again there are gender differences with 55 per cent of boys being able to perform five continuous skips at 66 months, which rises to 91 per cent of girls at the same time. Why these gender differences occur is open to debate, with discussions centring on preferences and participation in various types of activities but it is also clear that girls not only achieve more, but also hop and skip more smoothly and continuously.

Throwing

Throwing is a difficult skill to analyse because it can be done in different ways such as under-arm or over-arm, sideways, one or two hands. It is also probably true to say that the differences seen in throwing, particularly the overhand throw which is the one described here, are due both to biological make-up and socio cultural opportunities and expectations. This is particularly true of the gender differences that become apparent.

The overhand throw is a discrete movement involving a generation of force, direction to the object, timing of the release of the object and the maintenance of balance and posture following the throw. As babies approach their second birthday, they perform an action closely resembling a throw but it is crude, lacking in direction with little control of force. Early forms of the overhand throw are characterized by only the arm being involved with the feet remaining in place and no rotation of the trunk, probably aiding the child to keep postural control. The next phase involves some rotation of the trunk, and the arm moving to behind the head but with the feet still remaining stationary in position. The next phase involves much fuller trunk and leg movement with children taking a step forward to generate more power and stability at the end of the throw; often, however, in the first instance it is the 'wrong' leg, that is, the same side as the throwing arm is placed forward. A fuller mature throwing pattern does not occur until much later than our age range of early years, usually around 11 or 12, and involves a much more pronounced rotation of the trunk and a step forward with the contralateral leg.

A common observation is that more boys than girls reach this final stage, but we have little data to support this. As with many developmental progressions, throwing becomes smoother and looks easier with age and fewer extraneous movements are observed, alongside the seemingly paradoxical observation that more body parts are involved in more complex ways; however, the difference is that they are controlled, coordinated and involved directly in the throwing action. Detailed analysis of the developmental stages has been provided by Roberton (1977, 1978, 1984).

Balancing

Before about 30 months children's balance is not usually assessed in a formal manner but is seen as part of other activities such as control of posture. This continues and balance becomes part of everyday locomotor activities such as running, hopping, skipping, climbing etc., but also starts to receive attention in its own right and can be assessed directly. For example, children start to walk on balance beams and are asked to stand on one foot which they can briefly do around the time of their second birthday. Some of the accomplishments of young children in the area of balance indicate that at two years of age a child can briefly stand on one foot, can walk forward on a line on the floor; by three years of age the child can stand on one foot for around five seconds and can walk forwards

on a circular line on the floor; by five years of age the child can stand on
one foot for 10 seconds.

A different approach to these types of norms was taken by Keogh
(1969) and reported in Keogh and Sugden (1985), and rather than use
the traditional categories of static and dynamic balance, Keogh selected
tasks that required control of posture in various ways according to
whether the body was stationary or moving. Table 2.2 shows some of the
results with the percentage of children who can pass various tasks at the
age of five. It is interesting to note that in every case except hopping and
turning 90 degrees, girls have a higher percentage passing rate than
boys. Keogh and Sugden (1985) note that beyond five years of age these
type of tasks are limited in use because children can simply perform
them for longer periods of time or more of them, with the result often in
testing that when failure occurs it is not that the children cannot accomplish the task, but that they are bored and feel it is of little use. However,
it is obvious that balance develops beyond this age, with complex skills
such as skateboarding, riding a bicycle, dodging a playmate and being
involved in a host of complex activities that all require control of posture
or balance.

Manual skills

By the age of two years, children have reasonably well coordinated manual skills that involve the arm–hand linkage and can quite accurately place
their hand and arm where they wish and are becoming more dextrous in
their manipulation skills. Between two and six/seven years of age, they
become quite proficient using their manual skills for dressing, construction, writing and drawing, feeding and a host of other skills. It is at this
age that motor skills start to work within social constraints with, for example, it becoming more important how a child uses feeding implements,
not simply that s/he does so.

The manner in which manual skills were divided in the first part of the
chapter will be continued here within a framework set by Keogh and
Sugden (1985) who divided the area into self-help skills, construction
skills, writing and drawing skills and bimanual control. It is recognized
that this particular area can be divided in numerous ways but this way
allows functional skills to be examined in the developmental context.

Dressing is a self-help skill that most parents love to see achieved. By
around 32 months children can dress with supervision and without
supervision at 42 months (Table 2.3). Notable other achievements are the
putting on of shoes at 36 months and the tying of laces by 48 months.

Putting on garments is a rather complex skill that involves matching
the garment to the proper body parts and in an appropriate spatial

Table 2.3 Age of achievement of self-help skills

Task	Age (months)	Study
Pulls on a simple garment	24	Knobloch and
Puts on shoes	36	Pasamanick (1974)
Laces shoes	48	
Unbuttons accessible buttons	36	
Distinguishes fronts and backs of clothes	48	
Dresses and undresses with supervision	48	
Buttons up	36	Frankenburg and
Dresses with supervision	32	Dodds (1967)
Dresses without supervision	43	
Washes and dries hands and face	42	Knobloch and
Brushes teeth	48	Pasamanick (1974)
Handles cup well	21	
Inhibits overturning of spoon	24	Knobloch and
Feeds self, spills little	36	Pasamanick (1974)
Pours well from pitcher	36	

Source: Keogh and Sugden (1985, p. 77)

relationship. Items such as jackets are notorious for presenting problems, especially in children with movement difficulties described in Chapter 3. It is not simply the perceptual matching of the garment; once the dressing process has started there are rather subtle motor control issues to resolve such as moving the arm through a tight sweater or 'manipulating' the foot into a shoe.

Buttoning and tying of laces are tasks that present difficulties to most children at some time in their lives. Both involve manipulation by the fingers but tying laces has the added difficulty in that the objects are not fixed and are free to vary, thus presenting more difficult movement problems. Other tasks such as grooming involve the hand and arm but are not manipulation in the sense that the fingers are constantly moving. For example, combing hair involves the fingers in a relatively fixed position while the arm is spatially positioning the hand in relation to the hair and head. Other tasks such as face washing involve manipulation of the soap to build up a lather and then the application to the face with the whole of the hand.

Feeding is a skill that has many components and we do not have full sets of data on all of the skills that are part of this area. By 24 months the child has some control of spoon and cup; by 36 months, children can use a number of utensils and can pour into a cup; when children are a little older they can perform these tasks with fewer extraneous movements such as minimizing trunk and limb movements. One has only to examine in detail the perceptual, cognitive and motor processes that are involved in everyday feeding activities such as eating a bowl of cereal or the very difficult eating a boiled egg by first removing the top-something some adults find a challenge! Using a spoon is a complex activity that involves spatial and timing abilities plus the ability to orient the spoon to first the object, then transport it to the mouth and finally to place it in the mouth, all without spilling the contents.

A whole set of activities appear during this age period which come under the generic heading of construction skills. Earlier, it was noted that building blocks are used as an indicator of construction skills. As children develop, more sophisticated tasks can be attempted such as tool use where a spatial relationship is maintained between the tool and an object. It is often a unimanual skill but often an object is held with one hand while the other uses a tool. In a young child's environment hammers, screwdrivers and saws are used as well as scissors and similar tools.

Writing and drawing are two skills of major importance that develop between the ages of two and six/seven. By four years of age a child has a large repertoire of grips including the tripod grip which involves holding a pencil by the thumb, index finger and middle finger. This progresses through various stages before reaching the mature form and even then there are lots of variations on this. By 24 months children can make circular, vertical and horizontal lines but these are quite variable in quality. By 36 months children are able to draw a circle, at 48 months a cross, a square at 54 months, a triangle at 60 months and a triangle at 72 months. There is an interesting task involving the use of matchsticks and shapes. Children can make a shape such as a square with matchsticks before they can draw it with a pencil, indicating that the child has the concept of the shape but cannot continuously draw it, whereas making a shape with matchsticks allows continuous matching and changing of the position if necessary. When making a shape with a pencil, there is the continuous problem of keeping the representation in mind, making a plan and executing the motor problem.

Not all children will be ready to start writing as soon as they begin school, but as Sassoon (1990) points out, there are dangers in waiting too long and letting the children experiment for themselves. Writing is such a crucial skill, even in this age of computers, that it is essential to ensure children have correct and constant instruction. In Chapter 5, there are guidelines for instruction at this early age.

General coordination issues

Most of the descriptions so far have involved functional tasks in daily situations such as walking, jumping and reaching and grasping. It is possible to examine the basics of these by analysing some coordination tasks that

make demands upon the children not always seen in everyday life, iol-
lowed by tasks that involve children in attempting to produce maximum
effort, something that is constantly asked later in childhood. General coordination issues have been assessed by such tasks as opening and closing
hands either separately or together and we find that below five years of age
this is very difficult; by five, 22 per cent of boys can accomplish this with
hands together rising to 78 per cent by seven years of age. The comparable figures for girls are 43 per cent to 83 per cent. Another such task is
hopping in one place twice on one foot, switching while moving to twice
on the other foot. By five only 3 per cent of boys can accomplish this, rising to 48 per cent at seven, with the girls having respective passing rates of
16 per cent and 69 per cent. It is clear that for boys especially and girls,
this is a skill that still requires development. Overall, Keogh and Sugden
(1985) note that the girls were approximately one year ahead of the boys
and in addition, qualitatively showed more maturity by, for example, having softer movements and not having to monitor their movements all of
the time. Why girls do slightly better than boys has not been firmly established. It could be that girls are biologically more mature than boys; they
reach puberty earlier and are more advanced in skeletal development and
this is also reflected in the neuromotor system. Conversely, there is a cultural argument that girls are more likely to practise these skills.

Spatial and temporal accuracy

Much of what has been described so far has been in the context of 'closed'
movements. These are movements in which the child has control of when
to perform the task and to a lesser extent, where. When the child or more
crucially, the environment begins to move, creating an 'open' situation,
there are increasing demands upon the child with the spatial and temporal variables being outside of his/her control. Much of the work
performed on this area has been with children in the 5–12 age group as
below the age of five, open situations are very difficult for children.
However, it is something that is advocated as being part of any movement
experience in the early years as these are important in setting the foundations for future movement opportunities.

In Figure 2.5 there is a representation of the closed to open continuum according to the interaction between the mover and the environment.
As the mover changes from being in a stable to a moving situation, and as
any environment progresses from a stable to a changing situation, so the
overall context moves from closed to being open. With this progression,
the context is more unpredictable in both space and time.

Figure 2.6 illustrates this with the task of stepping and jumping. In the
first instance the context is at the more closed end of the continuum with

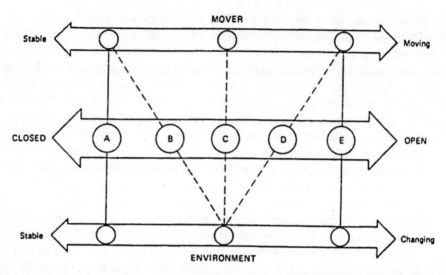

Figure 2.5 Continuum of closed-open situations. Source: Keogh and Sugden (1985, p. 105).

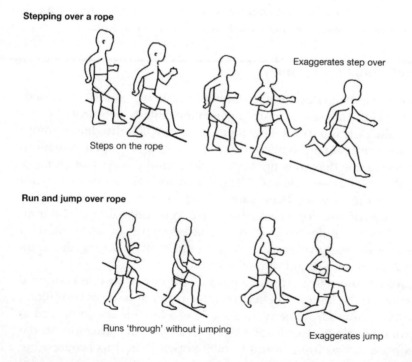

Figure 2.6 Movement variations in different rope-jump tasks. Source: Keogh and Sugden (1985, p. 100).

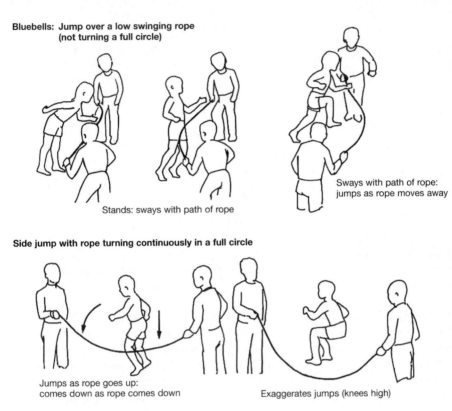

Bluebells: Jump over a low swinging rope (not turning a full circle)

Stands: sways with path of rope

Sways with path of rope: jumps as rope moves away

Side jump with rope turning continuously in a full circle

Jumps as rope goes up: comes down as rope comes down

Exaggerates jumps (knees high)

Figure 2.6 continued.

the rope static and the child being able to choose when to perform the relatively simple task of stepping over the rope. This progresses to a jump over a stationary rope and finally progresses to an open context where the child has to jump over a moving rope and not having control of either space or time in the action.

A good example of the progression in this area is shown in Figure 2.7 illustrating a study by Williams (1973) who projected a ball into the air but its flight after the initial part was occluded by a large canvas. Children were asked to watch the ball as far as they could and then run to the place they predicted the ball would land. All children could move in the appropriate direction but the younger children aged six to eight years had a mean error of 22 feet in predicting where the ball would land, compared to two and a half feet for nine to 12 year olds. Thus this ability to predict spatially in a contextual moving environment develops rapidly between eight and 12 years of age.

When examining temporal accuracy we find similar results. Smoll (1973) found a steady improvement in performance between the ages of 5 and 11 years. Bard et al. (1981) showed that errors in milliseconds for

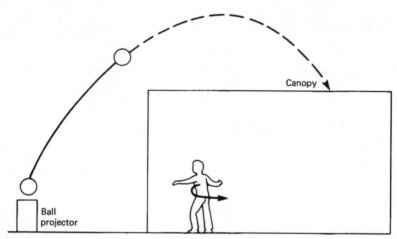

Figure 2.7 General representation of ball projected to land on overhead canopy with child moving to the spot where he thinks the ball will land. Source: Keogh and Sugden (1985, p. 114).

a coincident timing task, involving button pressing to intercept a moving target, decreased from 150 to around 60 between the ages of 6 and 11 years. Other studies by Dorfman (1977) and Wade (1980) confirm and extend the finding that this ability to intercept and coincide with a moving object improves greatly between the ages of 6 and 11 years. By the age of 3 children are becoming pretty competent in stable and closed situations, but they will have had limited opportunities for moving in open situations. Between 3 and 5 years opportunities start to present themselves but the real improvement appears to take place between the ages of 5–6 and 11 (Bard et al., 1990; Lefebvre and Reid, 1998). Although this only just overlaps with our age group, it does indicate that during the early years there should be preparation for this kind of activity and as will be outlined in the intervention chapter, activities will be encouraged that involve spatial and temporal predictions.

One important skill that involves both prediction and anticipation is catching. Even at a rudimentary level, a child has to make preparatory movements in advance of the object arriving. Developmental progressions often depend upon what is being thrown and in what manner. However, there are noticeable changes that occur if the object and manner of throwing is kept constant. In the early stages there is little anticipation with arms simply extended with the hands pointing upwards and the ball trapped against the chest. With development, anticipation and prediction occur with the arms starting to move under the ball and eventually the ball being caught solely by the hands which have adjusted to the flight and size of the ball. Alongside this upper limb progression, the body changes from being static to one that moves and adjusts to the flight of the incoming ball. An interesting exercise is to analyse a child's catching using observation of the arm, hand and body action components during the activity (Haywood and Getchell, 2001).

Concluding comments

The philosophy that is being adhered to in this book is that the development of motor skills is a crucial part of a child's overall development. If this is impaired or parts are missing, the child not only has difficulty in the everyday activities involving motor skills such as self-help skills, recreational activities, classroom practices but also there is a knock-on effect to other areas of the child's development as the overall progress presents an uneven profile. The logical progression from this is that an understanding of the development of motor skills is essential if detailed analysis and eventually, intervention is required. If one took a parallel analogy in the form of language development, it is commonplace to analyse the normal development of language skills in preparation for any intervention. The same should be true with motor skills although this kind of analysis is not as common.

In this chapter there has been a presentation of the normally developing child from birth through six or seven years of age, with the age band split into two; the birth-to-two-years-of-age group followed by the two-to-six-year-old group. In both cases, the development of motor skills has been described and analysed with a proposal as to why these skills change and develop. The ultimate aim is for those in contact with young children to have a strong knowledge of what is expected and why development takes place helping to arrange a context where the children have the opportunity to develop the crucial fundamental motor skills to provide them with a usable motor vocabulary by the time they are seven years of age.

CHAPTER 3

Movement skill difficulties

Introduction

Developmental Coordination Disorder (DCD) at its core is characterized by poor motor skills. Children with DCD have difficulties with motor coordination as compared with other children of the same age. These children have difficulties in mastering gross motor coordination tasks such as crawling, walking, jumping, standing on one foot, catching a ball and fine coordination task such as tying shoelaces. Some children also demonstrate expressive speech problems. *The essential feature of DCD is a marked impairment in the development of motor coordination.* Most of our information on DCD comes from work in the five- to eleven year old age range. The emphasis in this text is on three to six year olds taking a younger age period with concomitant different activities and range of skills.

The fundamental and core difficulty is that performance in daily activities requiring motor coordination is substantially below that expected given the person's chronological age and measured intelligence. This may be manifested by marked delays in achieving motor milestones (e.g. walking, crawling, sitting), dropping things, 'clumsiness', poor performance in sports, or poor handwriting (Criterion A, DSM IV, 1994; DSM IV TR, 2000). A second part of the definition is that the disturbance significantly interferes with academic achievement or activities of daily living (Criterion B). Two exclusionary clauses are also present in the definition. The first states that the disturbance is not due to a general medical condition (e.g. cerebral palsy, hemiplegia, or muscular dystrophy) and does not meet the criteria for a Pervasive Developmental Disorder (Criterion C) and, secondly, if Mental Retardation is present, the motor difficulties are in excess of those usually associated with it (Criterion D).

The prevalence rate for DCD has been estimated to be around 6 per cent (APA, DSM-IV, 1994; WHO, 1992) for children of 5–11 years of age though a more conservative estimate is somewhere around 4.5–5 per cent (Wright and Sugden, 1996a). In most studies the prevalence of boys is reported to be higher than that of girls, with a boy–girl ratio of at least 2:1 (Wright and Sugden, 1996a).

A common feature of children with DCD is difficulty in those motor skills necessary for progress in the formal and informal learning environment of school. The impaired ability to control functional movements often continues throughout the school years with evidence to show that, without intervention, these difficulties persist into later life (Cantell et al., 1994; Geuze and Börger, 1993; Gillberg et al., 1989; Losse et al., 1991) and that the earlier treatment can begin, the better the outcome (Cantell et al., 1994; Schoemaker et al., 1994).

During the last twenty to thirty years, DCD has received a great deal of attention from researchers in a number of fields including psychology, education, paediatrics, physiotherapy, occupational therapy and more recently sport and exercise science.

However, despite the increase in attention into DCD, there are still problems to be solved surrounding the classification of specific coordination disorders including terminology, diagnostic criteria, associated features and overlap with other disorders (Barnett et al., 1998). Additionally, Visser (2003) notes that the aetiology and prognosis of DCD are still unclear; children with DCD may show a variety of symptoms and their specific needs, as well as their prognosis, will differ accordingly. He states that if we are to understand the aetiology and prognosis of DCD, we need to have a better understanding of its nature. What complicates our understanding of the aetiology and prognosis of DCD is the comorbidity of motor difficulties and difficulties in other non-motor areas. Visser (2003) notes that many children diagnosed with DCD also display problems with attention and concentration or specific learning difficulties, such as dyslexia and specific language impairment.

Historical perspective

Since the beginning of the twentieth century, there have been case histories of children who have shown coordination difficulties such that they interfere with academic achievement and activities of daily living. In 1962 an article entitled 'Clumsy Children' appeared in the *British Medical Journal* which discussed behaviour seen in young schoolchildren that could mistakenly be attributed to naughtiness or low intelligence but was, according to the authors, more likely to be a consequence of poor motor control. This disorder, found not uncommonly in primary-school-aged children, resulted in a marked impairment in the performance of functional skills required to succeed at school. Impaired motor performance by this age group had been noticed prior to the publication of the paper in the *British Medical Journal*

(1962) but, as observed by Sugden and Wright (1998), this paper possibly marked the beginning of published works that adopted a scientific approach to the study of what is now recognized as *Developmental Coordination Disorder* (DCD). The paper called for concerted study to be undertaken to widen awareness of the condition, to diagnose precisely and thus to maximize opportunities to help these children.

Perhaps most notable of the early studies is that of Orton (1937); he described children who displayed strikingly similar characteristics to those children who are nowadays described as having DCD and noticed that poor motor performance often involved movements of the body as a whole, including such factors as balance and gait, in addition to manual dexterity. In 1962, Walton et al. observed a syndrome in five children in which the principle feature was described as 'severe clumsiness'. They noted that these children displayed clumsiness to such a degree that many motor activities essential to everyday life were distinctly impaired. A number of other earlier studies report similar finding to Walton et al. (1962) (Brenner and Gillman, 1966; Brenner et al., 1967; Dare and Gordon, 1970; Gubbay et al., 1965). In general, school performance was found to be poor, the children had been slower in attaining milestones in their development of motor skills, and a high proportion of them presented definite indications of clumsiness, speech defects or poor motor coordination.

As a clearer picture of the motor difficulties faced by children with DCD has emerged, interest and research in the subject has spread from medical personnel to psychologists, educationalists, and health therapists. Sugden and Wright (1998) note that these professionals are united not only in their quest for an understanding of the condition but also in how to deal with and help children overcome their difficulties. Over the last 40 years there has been a greater concentration of effort in research and clinical work in the area, perhaps typified by the establishment of a worldwide DCD group, which has held conferences since 1994 with a one-day meeting in London, England with 30–40 participants. The growth in interest is perhaps best illustrated by the 2005 DCD conference to be held in Trieste, Italy with over 180 participants, held over four days with many delegates from around the world.

Terminology

Many terms have been used to describe the condition and, as noted by Sugden and Wright (1998), the descriptors used often reflect the emphases of the researchers' interests and also shed light on the difficulties experienced by children with movement problems. The most common of the terms used is *clumsy children* (Dare and Gordon, 1970;

Geuze and Kalverboer, 1994; Henderson, 1994; Keogh et al., 1979; Lord and Hulme, 1987a; Losse et al., 1991). Other terms used include *clumsy child syndrome* (Gubbay, 1975a); *coordination problems* or *difficulties* (O'Beirne et al., 1994; Sugden and Henderson, 1994); *motor coordination problems* or *difficulties* (Maeland, 1992; Roussounis et al., 1987); *movement skill problems* (Sugden and Sugden, 1991); *movement problems* or *difficulties* (Henderson et al., 1989; Sugden and Keogh, 1990; Wright et al. 1994); *perceptuo-motor dysfunction* (Laszlo et al., 1988a); *dyspraxia* (Iloeje, 1987; McGovern, 1991; Walton et al., 1962).

The most recent and formal term used to describe these children is *Developmental Coordination Disorder* (DCD). It appears in both the American Psychiatric Association (APA) *Diagnostic and Statistical Manual for Mental Disorders* (DSM-III-R, 1987; DSM-IV, 1994; DSM-IV-TR, 2000) and the World Health Organization (WHO) *International Classification of Diseases and Related Health Problems* (ICD-10, 1992a; 1992b; 1993), and was first classified as such in DSM-III-R (1978). The classification in these manuals represents a very positive step forward, not only in terms of recognition of the disorder but also because of the credibility these manuals offer. Henderson (1994) notes that the fact that DCD now has a specific entry and is regarded as a separable developmental disorder of movement skills means that it requires diagnostic, aetiological and remedial attention in its own right. The term *Developmental Coordination Disorder* has also been used, among others, by Henderson (1992, 1994); Hoare (1994); Missiuna (1994); Mon-Williams et al. (1994); Polatajko et al. (1995a, b); Sugden and Wright (1996, 1998).

Core characteristics

It is generally acknowledged that there is much variation in the way movement skill difficulties manifest themselves in the early years of life, but some core characteristics have been identified. The American Psychiatric Association description of DCD has been noted above while the World Health Organization (ICD-10, 1992a) describes the features of Specific Developmental Disorder of motor dysfunction as

A disorder in which the main feature is a serious impairment in the development of motor coordination that is not solely explicable in terms of general intellectual retardation or any specific congenital or acquired neurological disorder. Nevertheless, in most cases a careful clinical examination shows marked neurodevelopmental immaturities such as choreiform movements of unsupported limbs or mirror movements and other associated motor features, as well as signs of impaired fine and gross motor coordination. (WHO, 1992a, F82)

The extent to which the earlier noted descriptors differ is a testament to the heterogeneity of the difficulties experienced by children with DCD. Wright and Sugden (1996a) note that not only are the differences in children revealed in their range, but also the pervasiveness of the problem differs from child to child. For some children, their difficulties may only be evident in fine motor tasks or in gross motor tasks. For some, the difficulties they experience may be due to the environment, in that it limits or affords the child's movement control. For other children, their lack of motor control is evident in every area, and, as noted by Hoare (1994) and Wright and Sugden (1996b), variability of severity is evident in this situation also. These difficulties could arise from difficulty in task execution, poor planning of motor tasks, a lack of understanding, or a cognitive difficulty with the task and how it fits in with other movements.

The overall picture of children with DCD shows that the basic fundamental skills of sitting, standing, walking, running, reaching and grasping always emerge even though they may be delayed. However, although these skills can be performed at a rudimentary level, the necessary development to competent functional skills has not occurred (Henderson, 1992; Keogh and Sugden, 1985; Sugden and Henderson, 1994). Sugden and Henderson (1994) suggest that this lack of development means that, in comparison, children with DCD fall behind their peers in some or all of these functional skills, resulting in a detrimental effect on their progress at school.

Prevalence

According to DSM-III-R (1987), DSM-IV (1994) and DSM-IV-TR (2000) a prevalence of DCD as high as 6 per cent has been estimated for children of 5–11 years of age. Other studies from around the world lend weight to this estimation. Gubbay (1975a) found up to 6.1 per cent of a population of almost a thousand school children to be *clumsy*. Keogh et al. (1979), using multiple procedures, identified 9 per cent of six-year-old boys as *clumsy*. Later studies have also found similar percentages. Henderson and Hall (1982) found 5 per cent of a sample of 400 children displaying *developmental clumsiness*, Iloeje (1987) found a prevalence rate of 5.9 per cent of Nigerian children with *developmental apraxia*. Henderson et al. (1992) reported that it has been estimated that up to 10 per cent of school age children may suffer from DCD, exhibiting *clumsiness* that is not due to an intellectual deficit or identifiable physical disorder. Wright et al. (1994) identified 4.72 per cent of children in Singapore as having definite movement problems and a further 10.85 per cent classified as being at risk.

However, in spite of the apparent agreement of prevalence, these figures are subject to definitional difficulties and the use of different instruments to identify children with DCD. When prevalence figures are published it is not simply a question of whether they agree with other figures, but also whether the same children are being assessed. This often varies according to how and for what purpose children are being assessed. For example, Maeland (1992) pointed out that although three different assessment methods identified about the same amount of children (5–5.6 per cent), each procedure identified a different set of children. Henderson and Sugden (1992) in the Manual for the Movement ABC state that below the 5th percentile a child is most likely to have coordination difficulties that require immediate attention and those from the 5th percentile to 15th percentile are considered 'at risk' and should be monitored accordingly.

Sugden and Henderson (1994) observe that in most studies the prevalence of boys is higher than that of girls, with some showing a slight difference while in others the ratio is as high as 3:1. Wright and Sugden (1996a) found similar prevalence rates among 6- to 9-year-old children in Singapore. The reasons for the higher prevalence rate among boys are unclear, but Sugden and Henderson (1994) point out that similar ratios are reported for children who suffer from other specific learning difficulties such as dyslexia and ADHD.

Nature of DCD

The knowledge gained over the past 30 years or so has been extensive, but the exact nature of DCD from the literature has not yet reached the point where a totally clear picture is presented (Sugden and Wright, 1998). Individual aspects of the disorder have been researched, highlighting distinctive behaviours; however, reports can be seen to reveal the perspective and interest of the author and it is generally believed that the assessment and testing procedures influence what is found. Not only can the assessment procedures bias the findings in a certain direction, but the methods chosen to report the findings may also have an effect. However, despite these cautious reservations, some characteristics are evident.

Two procedures have been used to investigate the nature of DCD. The first is to compare the behaviours of children with DCD with those of children not displaying the characteristics of DCD. This method follows a long-established tradition of intergroup analysis, and distinctive aspects of DCD investigated in this way are well documented. However, an underlying question when performing intergroup analysis involves the concept of a syndrome; are differences found between DCD and non-DCD children clear, consistent and reliable enough to constitute a recognizable syndrome? This involves the issue of homogeneity and whether children with DCD form a homogeneous group. Sugden and Keogh (1990) and Sugden and Sugden (1991) observed that, far too often, children with DCD are treated as a homogeneous group with respect to characteristics and remediation. However, recent research has shown that these children do not form a homogeneous group, and various attempts have been made to discover the exact nature of DCD. Wright and Sugden (1996b) demonstrated that there are two distinct methods of assessing the nature of DCD; *intergroup characteristics*, in which children with DCD are clearly different from a control group and *intragroup characteristics*, where difficulties seen within the DCD group are not common to all the children.

What are the differences between a DCD group and one without DCD?

A number of studies have noted the differences between children with DCD and those without. One of the first was that noted by the *British Medical Journal* (1962) which lists many characteristics of children who are 'clumsy'; these characteristics include being in trouble at school, bad behaviour, experiencing difficulties with self-help skills and being awkward in their movements. A further study by Walton et al. (1962), found that the clumsy children displayed

> excessive clumsiness of movement, poor topographical orientation, inability to draw, to write easily and to copy. (p. 610)

In a study by Gubbay (1975b), children described as *clumsy* and matched controls were assessed on a screening test which consisted of eight motor skills tasks and a questionnaire which was completed by the children's teachers. Gubbay found that the *clumsy* children differed significantly from the controls on almost all the motor skills tasks; tasks such as handwriting, sporting ability, academic performance, behaviour and general motor skills.

Sugden and Wright (1998) note that during the 1970s and early 1980s, papers were produced that continued to demonstrate the difficulties that children with DCD experienced in comparison with other children. These papers demonstrated a sophistication not seen before, and provided information gained in a scientific manner. One such study is that by Keogh et al. (1979), who considered whether different teachers and educators would identify clumsiness with any consistency. The children were assessed by a teacher-rated Checklist, classroom observations and a motor skills test. Another study by Roussounis et al. (1987) describes the poor results on a standardized test of motor performance that children with

DCD achieved in relation to their general abilities. Both these papers used standardized tests and the inclusion of control subjects with which to compare results.

A further study by Henderson and Hall (1982) investigated the characteristics of *clumsy* children compared with matched controls. The children were assessed with a battery of tests which included a motor impairment test, neurodevelopmental examinations, ratings of children's drawings, and an IQ and reading test. A particular focus within the study was to explore the possibility of subgroups within the DCD group. Henderson and Hall (1982) used the term *subgroup* to describe distinct behaviours seen within the DCD group, such as children whose motor impairment was an isolated problem from their IQ, reading and number work. Another group included children whose motor impairment was associated with a number of other problems, such as low academic attainment, social immaturity, and negative attitudes toward school.

Research in this area continues to use matched controls to examine the differences between children displaying characteristics of DCD and non-DCD children but it has now moved on to isolate behaviours in a laboratory setting with greater control of confounding variables to assess aspects of DCD.

Sensory/perceptual functioning

Some researchers have looked at the differences between a sample of *clumsy* children and a matching control group on their ability to process sensory/perceptual information. In a series of studies, Hulme and colleagues investigated the processing of visual and kinaesthetic information in children with DCD (Hulme et al., 1982a, b; Hulme et al., 1984; Lord and Hulme, 1987a, 1987b, 1988). In all these studies it was found that children with DCD made poorer visual and kinaesthetic judgements than control children. Hulme and his colleagues also found that the children's poor performance on the visual tasks correlated with their poor movement skill, leading them to suggest that a deficit in visual processing is a causal factor in children with DCD.

In a follow-up study, Lord and Hulme (1987a) presented results that indicated a serious deficit in perceptual processing in children with DCD. Visual acuity was tested to rule out visual-sensory impairments and, accordingly, it was found that the children with DCD displayed no problems in this respect. However, in each of the tests administered to assess visuospatial perception, there were significant differences between the control children and those with DCD.

Mon-Williams et al. (1994) studied ophthalmic function in children with DCD and explored the possibility that visual impairments contribute to the problems of children with DCD. Results indicated that there were no significant abnormalities within the DCD group, suggesting that motor problems can exist even with perfect retinal image clarity. However, the authors point out that visual processing consists of much more than the provision of a clear retinal image and a deficit may lie elsewhere within the visual processing system. They further observe that these results lend weight to Abernethy's theory (1986) that ophthalmic factors play but a minor role in the control of perceptual-motor actions. They conclude that simple ophthalmic problems are not a causal factor in the motor difficulties experienced by children with DCD.

Dwyer and McKenzie (1994) studied the role of visual memory in the development of motor coordination. Their results suggest that children with DCD are unable to employ efficient rehearsal strategies to maintain a visual image in a form that would enable them to act upon it. In a follow-up study, Skorji and McKenzie (1997) examined the ability of children with DCD to reproduce short sequences of simple movements. Their findings for immediate recall replicated those of Dwyer and McKenzie (1994). However, when interference dimensions were introduced in the recall tests, children with DCD differed from the control children when visual interference with a high spatial involvement was presented, leading the authors to suggest that children with DCD are more dependent on visuospatial rehearsal when memorizing modelled movements.

In more recent studies, Sigmundsson et al. (2003) found that 'clumsy' children were significantly less sensitive than control children on a number of tasks of visual sensitivity. Schoemaker et al (2001) investigated whether children with DCD experience problems in the processing of visual, proprioceptive or tactile information. On a manual pointing task, they found that children with DCD made inconsistent responses towards the target in all three conditions. Similarly, Estil et al. (2002) examined ball catching and found a control group to be better than children with DCD with respect to both spatial and temporal performance in intercepting a moving ball.

Kinaesthetic functioning

Research work in the motor control area has shown that kinaesthetic or proprioceptive functioning is an important variable of learning motor skills. Laszlo and colleagues (Laszlo and Bairstow, 1985; Laszlo et al., 1988a, 1998b) used a process-orientated approach to investigate the nature of DCD in respect to diagnosis and treatment. Much of their work has centred on the contribution of kinaesthesis to motor control and the Kinaesthetic Sensitivity Test (KST) (Laszlo and Bairstow, 1985). Their work emphasized the poor results seen in children with DCD on tasks that included kinaesthetic acuity, perception, memory, and velocity discrimination. After kinaesthetic training, the children with DCD made significant improvement in motor skill performance thus demonstrating the significant role of kinaesthetic sensitivity in motor control (Laszlo et al. 1988a, 1998b).

Other work coming from the work of Laszlo and colleagues is reported by Sims and colleagues (Sims et al., 1996a, b). In the first study, Sims et al. (1996a) found no differential effect between two groups of children with DCD, when one group received kinaesthetic training and the other group was offered no treatment. In the second study, Sims et al. (1996b) compared three groups of children; one received kinaesthetic training, one received a programme of treatment specifically designed to avoid any reference to kinaesthetic training, and one group received no intervention. Children who received no treatment did not improve their performance, whereas both groups of children receiving help improved significantly; however, neither group improved more than the other.

Other researchers have also found contrary evidence to that reported by Laszlo (1988a, 1998b). Similarly to Sims et al. (1996a; 1996b), Sugden and Wann (1987) and Polatajko et al. (1995b) did not find a significant relationship between the KST (Laszlo and Bairstow, 1985) and a normative-based test of motor impairment, finding that children who received KST training did not perform any differently from other groups of children. Both these studies suggest that increased kinaesthetic acuity does not immediately translate into increased motor performance and neither does it generalize into new found skills.

Information processing and motor programming

Another way of investigating and assessing DCD has been to employ an information processing model, concentrating on the role of feedback and motor programming. Lord and Hulme (1988) found that when children with DCD were compared with a group of children not displaying DCD on a rotary pursuit tracking task, the children with DCD were poorer performers when time on target was considered, although patterns of movement were similar between the two groups. Lord and Hulme (1988) concluded that although the children with DCD were not limited by an ability to develop a motor programme, they were restricted by impaired visual feedback control. They suggested that although children with DCD have a representation of what needs to be done, they are slow in processing information that affects other aspects of motor control.

Smyth and Glencross (1986) suggested that children with DCD are deficient in speed of processing kinaesthetic information but not in speed of processing visual information. Their findings suggested that DCD is associated with a dysfunction in proprioceptive information processing but not with an impairment in the response selection process. Further, in a study by Smyth and Mason (1997), differences were found between children with DCD and a control group on their ability to use proprioceptive information to match postures and to map between visual and proprioceptive space and between targets defined by the felt positions of their two arms. However, it was noted that the same children displayed no differences in planning for end state comfort. Smyth and Mason (1997) conclude that the inability to carry out simple motor tasks predicts difficulties with proprioceptive matching and aiming, but does not predict performance on action planning.

van der Meulen et al (1991) supported the findings of Smyth and Glencross (1986) and found only small differences between children with DCD and their matched controls in their abilities to process visual feedback. van der Meulen and colleagues (1991) suggested that the increased time delay the children with DCD showed when trying to track a target was a consequence of a strategy they employed to deal with their difficulties in motor performance, and was not due to impaired information processing. Similarly, Wann (1987) found that children experiencing problems with handwriting employed movements that allowed greater visual control during movement execution. Sugden and Wright (1998) note that this can be seen as a strategy used to compensate for difficulties in motor performance, with a need to rely more heavily on visual feedback from the writing movements.

Rösblad and von Hofsten (1994) further assessed the role of vision in the guidance of movement and explored the possibility that children with DCD may be more dependent on vision than other children. Although all children were affected by removal of vision, the children with DCD did not appear to be especially disturbed. However, Rösblad and von Hofsten (1994) found that the time taken for the children with DCD was slower than for the controls, suggesting that the children with DCD were no more or less reliant on visual feedback to control their movements; both groups slowed down the movement to maintain their accuracy level. The initial slower and more variable movements of the children with DCD is not then attributable to visual information but could possibly result from poor forward planning. If a child finds it difficult to plan ahead or anticipate and prepare for difficulties, then errors have to be dealt with as they occur, which interrupts the smoothness and efficiency of movement. Rösblad and von Hofsten (1994) conclude that this strategy is the result of anticipatory monitoring being replaced with feedback monitoring, which is slower and more variable. The impaired capacity for anticipatory control is seen as a limiting factor for children with DCD.

Sugden and Wright (1998) note that these papers appear to agree that children with DCD have slower movements than their matched controls but each paper offers slightly different explanations for this. Explanations range from regarding perceptual aspects of the information-processing model as impaired to aspects of processing that link the input of information to the cognitive aspects of information processing. The intertwined role of these two features of information processing, input and decision making, appears to be significant.

Other studies have considered the central decision-making capacity of children with DCD. van Dellen and Geuze (1988) found that children with DCD were slower to respond to stimuli but not inaccurate in their movements; they concluded that the slowness was largely the result of an impaired cognitive decision process response selection. In a second study, van Dellen and Geuze (1990) found that when the movement accuracy demands were relatively high, children with DCD were slower than controls in executing simple, goal-directed hand movements. This finding was replicated by Vaessen and Kalverboer (1990) who found that motor tasks requiring greater accuracy created a heavier load for children with DCD than motor tasks with time pressures. Sugden and Wright (1998) suggest that it is possible that children with DCD underestimate the requirements of the higher movement accuracy demands and, as a result, need more time to adjust their inappropriate movements. This could be due to inaccuracy in the perception of the accuracy demands or inaccuracy in the planning or programming of such movements.

In a similar vein, Henderson et al. (1992) found that children with DCD perform less well than control children in tasks with both a cognitive and a motor load. Henderson and colleagues (1992) found that it was not the motor loading that caused the decrement in performance but rather the cognitive loading in terms of the increased accuracy demands made by the reaction time task.

The findings of the studies concerning DCD and information processing suggest that there is evidence of visual and kinaesthetic deficits in children with DCD, specifically concerning the input aspect of the information-processing model, leading to difficulties in error detection and movement correction during execution, resulting in less efficient motor programming in children with DCD, especially when accuracy and anticipation is required. As the complexity and spatial uncertainty of tasks increases, children with DCD find more and more difficulties with motor control.

These studies have all used matched controls to highlight the differences between two groups of children, and it is widely believed that detailed, pertinent information can be gained about impaired processes from research using this experimental design. Henderson (1992) notes that each separate study advances the knowledge and understanding of what underlies DCD but whether it will ever be possible to produce a cohesive theoretical account from such divergent sources remains unclear.

What are the differences within a DCD group?

An inherent presumption in the above method of investigation is that children with DCD all demonstrate the behaviours in question. Experimental designs including control children that have made group-based findings on a variety of characteristics of children with DCD appear to concur and, in some papers, there is a suggestion that the nature of DCD is such that the impairments seen in some children are not evident in others. This section attempts to show that children with DCD differ sufficiently from within their own groupings to warrant *intragroup* analysis of this disorder.

A number of studies exist which identify children with DCD as forming a heterogeneous group, in that the movement patterns they display are different in different children (Barnett and Henderson, 1992; Cantell et al., 1994; Dare and Gordon, 1970; Dewey and Kaplan, 1994; Gubbay, 1975b; Henderson and Hall, 1982; Hoare, 1994; Sugden and Sugden, 1991; Wright, 1996; Wright and Sugden, 1996a, 1996b, 1996c). In addition, Sugden and Chambers (2003) have suggested that the differential response of children with DCD to an intervention programme may be an indication of the heterogeneity of the condition.

The extent to which the children experience movement difficulties is the factor that is most commonly used to discriminate one subgroup of children from another. Sugden and Sugden (1991) use the notion of children *at risk* and children with *movement problems* when referring to the severity of the disorder. The cut-off points in norm-referenced tests, such as the Movement Assessment Battery for Children (Movement ABC) (Henderson and Sugden, 1992), offer an indication of the severity by reference to percentile charts. It is possible, however, to place children with DCD in subgroups from within the group on the basis of severity and on the nature of the disorder.

Subtypes of DCD

The most comprehensive reports detailing subgroups of children with DCD are those by Dewey and Kaplan (1994), Hoare (1994), Wright and Sugden (1996b) and Miyahara (1994). Hoare (1994) reported on subgroups of children with DCD by examining the results of the children's performance on kinaesthetic, visual, cross modal (kinaesthetic and visual), and fine motor and gross motor tasks. Using cluster analysis, she confirmed heterogeneity within the DCD group and was able to define five patterns of impairment. From these patterns of impairment, Hoare (1994) was able to isolate five subgroups of children with DCD. One group found motor tasks difficult in the absence of perceptual problems, while another group had difficulties across both motor and perceptual domains. A third group had difficulties with both kinaesthetic and visual tasks, suggesting a generalized perceptual dysfunction. The children in the fourth group were characterized by their particularly good kinaesthetic processing but displayed a large difference between their performance on the visual and kinaesthetic tasks. A fifth group had a mixed profile, suggesting some separation of inability within the gross motor domain.

Hoare (1994) concluded that while these results demonstrate that the children with DCD all experienced difficulties with their movements, there were examples of where specific difficulties were far more evident within one subgroup than another. Although Hoare (1994) does not claim to have discovered consistent subgrouping of the disorder, she demonstrates the heterogeneity of children with DCD.

In the study by Dewey and Kaplan (1994), four subgroups were identified including a control group showing no motor problems. The four subgroups included one group with deficits in balance, coordination and gestural performance; one with deficits in motor sequencing; one with severe deficits evident in all areas, and one with no difficulties compared with the others. Of particular interest in this study is the distinction between the first two groups; one displaying difficulties in the execution of motor skills with planning apparently remaining intact, and one group showing difficulties in the planning.

The work of Hoare (1994) has been supported by Wright and Sugden (1996b); they found four clusters of children who, whilst all experiencing difficulties generally, had specific problems areas. The children in the first cluster demonstrated the most even profile of all the clusters and represented the least impaired of the DCD children; they needed help in all areas but their difficulties were not as severe as some of the other DCD children. The second cluster of children scored poorly on the factor indicating that help was needed to perform throwing, aiming, and receiving. The third cluster needed most assistance when the environment was changing, but they also exhibited difficulties in the *control of self* factor. The children in the fourth cluster demonstrated the most obvious difficulty; they recorded the highest score on manual tasks and the highest score for *dynamic balance*.

The clusters found by Wright and Sugden (1996b) matched some of those found by Hoare (1994), who also identified one group of children with a specific difficulty concerned with visually loaded tasks. Hoare (1994) also isolated a group of children who showed great difficulty with manual dexterity and with static and dynamic balance.

The cluster analysis used by Hoare (1994) found clusters of children with DCD who, although being equally impaired overall, demonstrated deficits that generalized across modalities and deficits that were highly specific. All the children in the Wright and Sugden (1996b) study were assessed using the Movement ABC (Henderson and Sugden, 1992) and failed either or both the Checklist or test, placing them in the DCD category. However, the factor and cluster analysis has shown that although they may be equally impaired according to test scores, they do not all demonstrate impairments in the same problematic motor behaviours.

The study by Wright and Sugden (1996b) also reveals some patterns of associated behaviours. Those children in cluster 3, considered to be the group with many difficulties, show the clearest pattern of associated behaviours related to their movement difficulties (as demonstrated by Section 5 of the Movement ABC Checklist, Henderson and Sugden, 1992); they are seen to be easily distracted, lacking in persistence, disorganized, and confused about their school tasks. As this group of children scored poorly on the *changing environment* factor, the associated behaviours would interact to make adjustments to a changing environment difficult. Cluster 4 also shows a profile of being easily distracted, looking around and responding to noise and movement outside of the classroom environment. Wright and Sugden (1996b) suggest that these associated behaviours may add to the poor performance in manual dexterity tasks done under a time constraint.

In a study also investigating the identification of subtypes of DCD, Miyahara (1994) concentrated on children with differing motor abilities who have a learning disability. While noting that this study has important implications for identifying subtypes of DCD, Macnab et al. (2001) comment that the restriction of the sample to children with a learning disability prevents any generalization of the result to the DCD population.

Macnab et al. (2001) have undertaken a study investigating the value of cluster analysis in the search for subtypes of DCD. The study looks in detail at three cluster analysis studies, namely those by Dewey and Kaplan (1994), Hoare (1994) and Miyahara (1994). The authors conclude that cluster analysis is a useful tool in the identification of subtypes of DCD but stress that it is imperative that the selection of variables should be guided by a clearly stated theoretical framework.

What is clear from these studies on subtypes is that not enough work has been conducted to determine stable subtypes of children with DCD. What is also clear is that the children have different profiles and, as noted by Sugden and Chambers (2003), these may have important implications for designing programmes of activities and strategies for intervention. A recent study by Kirby et al. (in preparation) presents a different way to examine intragroup differences by simply examining profiles of scores on the Movement ABC (Henderson and Sugden, 1992).

A further interesting approach to intra group differences was described by Sugden and Chambers (2003) who found that following a period of intervention, children with DCD not only differed in the final outcomes in their responses to intervention, but also the manner in which they progressed throughout the period of the intervention. Four loosely defined groups emerged: first, one which had adequate practice sessions and made significant gains-this being by far the biggest group; a second who made gains despite small amounts of practice; a third group who had little practice and made little progress; and finally a very small number who despite adequate intervention made little progress. In addition, those who made the substantial gains did so at different times during the intervention period, with some making gains in the first eight weeks and another group not changing until late on in the second eight weeks. This type of analysis would appear to be a fruitful ground for further study.

What does development look like through childhood?

The literature on stability or change in children with movement difficulties ranges from predictions between neurological examinations early in life to signs at school entry (Drillien and Drummond, 1983; Hall et al., 1995; Nichols and Chen, 1981) through school age predictions (Gillberg and Gillberg, 1983; Gillberg et al., 1989; Hellgren et al., 1993) to an examination of the condition later in life (Cantell et al., 1994). A small number of children appear to recover from an early diagnosis but in many others the DCD condition remains and/or associated features such as behaviour, cognitive or self-esteem problems arise in its place.

When examining origins and development, there are a number of age-related issues that need consideration. Stanley and Alberman (1984) noted that if there is a cohort of children with low birth weight and a short gestational age, there will be a higher incidence of children with cerebral palsy. However, the question arises about the remainder of the cohort who do not develop cerebral palsy; if these children are examined on entry into school, at around five years of age, will there be a higher incidence of general motor disorders? Sugden and Wright (1998) consider this and comment that an investigator can begin by identifying and assessing children for motor difficulties at five or six years of age and follow them longitudinally to monitor their development over the next few years. Are the same children identified at, for example, 12 or 16 years of age as those who were identified at five or six years of age? For those who remained the same, were there any experiences that they missed during childhood that may have contributed to any lack of improvement? Of equal importance is to examine children who were having problems at one age and yet these problems seemingly disappear a few years later.

There are two bodies of literature that deal with these questions. The first often concerns antecedents in the early years, such as birth factors, the status of the young infant, and development in the early years. The second body of literature examines the relationship between early school age motor disorders and the progression during the school years into adolescence.

Development in the early years

The relationship between neurological examinations and fundamental units early in life and later behavioural signs at school age has long been a concern of investigators. A number of longitudinal studies have investigated the first five years of life, examining the progression of children showing at-risk signs at birth to determine the predictive value of certain antecedent conditions.

A major study examining longitudinal data on young children was provided by a developmental screening programme conducted by Drillien and Drummond (1983) in Scotland. They examined the course and occurrence of neurodevelopmental disabilities during the first three years of life in relation to educational and behavioural problems during the first two years of schooling. 1.8 per cent of a population of 3667 children were found to have movement disorders as the primary problem. In addition, information was available on 100 children who were referred for displaying movement disorders. Of these, almost 40 could be placed in categories other than the primary disorder of a movement problem. It is interesting to note that 80 per cent of movement disorders were identified between 8 and 20 weeks, whereas only approximately 30 per cent of other problems were identified at this early stage. Sugden and Keogh (1990) comment that movement behaviours are the most notable response with the result that movement problems are more likely to be noted, often as indicators of other conditions. In the Drillien and Drummond (1983) study, many children with movement disorders also had minor abnormal neurological signs in the first three years. However, as noted by Sugden and Wright (1998), as there was an overall high proportion of children with minor abnormal neurological signs in the first year, having movement difficulties was too common a problem to be a predictor of other problems.

Hall and colleagues (1995) looked at motor function of children at eight years of age in a population of children who had very low birth weights. Using the Movement ABC (Henderson and Sugden, 1992), the authors found significant differences between children who had low birth weights and the control groups. Similar results were found by Roth et al. (1994) who examined neurodevelopmental status at one, four, and eight years of age and found that neurodevelopmental difficulties at one year of age are good predictors of outcome at eight years of age.

Some children identified at birth or shortly afterwards will continue to have motor problems later on. However, individual prediction is difficult. Group data will support the contention that a greater proportion of those with early problems will persist in showing them later in childhood. However, the data are not strong enough to take individual cases and make accurate predictions about future performance. This is made more complex by the measures that are taken at birth. From a group of children with neurological signs at birth, some may not survive, while others will develop recognized biological disorders, such as cerebral palsy. From the remainder, there will be a higher incidence of coordination disorders that persist through to school entry and may possibly continue through child-hood into adolescence.

Development from early school years to adolescence

There are two types of studies that provide information about develop-ment and progression from six or seven years of age onward, and it is from these that trends and principles can be drawn out. There are longi-tudinal studies which focus on general development, examining a number of variables including motor behaviour and there are studies that have specifically targeted motor behaviour, usually starting around six or seven years of age and which examine a group over a period of time.

Follow-up studies

A study entitled 'Clumsiness in Children: do they grow out of it?' was pub-lished by Losse et al. in 1991, in which the authors investigated the long-term prognosis for children with DCD. The study was a ten-year fol-low-up of a sample of 32 children, 16 of whom were originally described as *clumsy* and 16 children matched for age, gender, and intelligence. Ten years later, the authors carried out a series of assessments on all 32 chil-dren, including a neurodevelopmental test battery, The Henderson revision of the TOMI, Weschler Intelligence Scale for Children, a Perceived Competence Scale for Children, school records and an interest questionnaire and interview.

One of the questions addressed by this study concerned the changes within the DCD group over time. The data collected suggest that the chil-dren as a group tend to have pervasive problems in most areas, although many individual differences were noted. The scores on the motor assess-ment showed a general lack of proficiency and these were substantiated by comments from the pupils concerning their experiences. The academic and social competence scores are more variable; some were adequate, but overall they were more negative than they had anticipated. The authors presented results as case studies, one of which showed a child who was fairly successful at an early age but at 16 had a very low self-concept with plummeting IQ scores, achievement in school was very low, and had a serious emotional and behavioural difficulty. Another child from the DCD group still appeared to have motor difficulties, but he had supportive parents and teachers and was still highly motivated to learn new skills. This child did not have a low self-concept, his behaviour was good, and he was confident. Although his academic achievements were not high, he had many friends and appeared to be a well-adjusted teenager.

While noting that some earlier studies investigating this same question reveal difficulties, Losse and colleagues (1991) concluded from their own study that motor coordination disorders are not confined to early childhood, as most of the children in the DCD group still had coordination difficulties as teenagers. Losse et al. (1991) also concluded that the problems associated with poor motor skills at age six are still present at the age of 16, appearing to be true both for academic achievement and for social and emotional adaptation. However, they were cautious in interpreting these associated difficulties as being a direct consequence of motor coordination difficulties. Overall, Losse et al. (1991) noted that minor motor difficulties in early childhood should not be ignored; the effects of being poorly coordinated are evident into the teenage years and manifest themselves not only in the motor domain but also in other areas, affecting other aspects of the child's functioning.

Another follow-up study was reported by Cantell et al. (1994) who examined Finnish children at 15 years of age, having originally been diagnosed as motor delayed at five. At 15 years of age, the children were assessed on motor abilities, educational performance, social and emotional development including self-image, and leisure activities. The original cohort consisted of 106 children classified as motor delayed and 40 control children. For this study 10 years later, a total of 81 of the motor delayed children and 34 control children were found. Of the 81 motor delayed children, 53 were still classified as motor delayed and thus labelled the *stable clumsy* group, while 28 were found to be no longer different from the controls, and reclassified as the *intermediate group*. Of the children identified at five years of age, 46 per cent were still significantly different from the control group at 15. The intermediate group had some residual problems, such as being different from the control group on some tasks and not on others, but their overall performance was better than that of the stable *clumsy* group.

The *clumsy* group was found to have lower achievement but it was noted that this did not alter during the course of the study. They also displayed lower aspirations for their future and were also fairly accurate in their estimations of their performance at school. This group did not perceive their social status to be any different from the other groups but they took part in fewer social activities. The intermediate group continued to have some difficulties with motor tasks at 15, although these were less extreme than those found in the stable *clumsy* group. The intermediate group appeared to have adjusted to their difficulties and were succeeding in school and took part in sports and other social activities. Cantell and colleagues (1994) commented that the differences between this group and the stable *clumsy* group suggest that social and educational outcomes are poorest for those with the most extreme motor difficulties at five years of age or for those with motor difficulties associated with lower intellectual abilities. Cantell et al. (1994) concluded that

Some children do 'grow out of it;' some do not. (p. 127)

In a series of studies, Gillberg and Gillberg and colleagues identified a condition they have termed DAMP – deficits in attention, motor control and perception (Gillberg, 1983; Gillberg and Rasmussen, 1982a, 1982b; Gillberg et al., 1982; Gillberg, 1985; Gillberg and Gillberg, 1983, 1989; Gillberg et al., 1989). In Sweden, children are screened for DAMP at six years of age and many of these children have been followed through a number of longitudinal studies. Through these studies, the concept has been shown to be a pervasive disorder with both attention and behaviour deficits remaining with the children (Gillberg and Gillberg, 1983; Gillberg et al., 1989).

In their longitudinal study, Gillberg et al. (1989) found that from the age of seven to 13 years of age, 70 per cent of the original cohort of children with *motor perception dysfunction* (MPD) no longer displayed any characteristics. However, Gillberg and Gillberg (1989), reporting on the same cohort of children, found that 84 per cent of the children still classified as having MPD had either behavioural or school achievement problems at 13 years of age.

Using the same children, Hellgren et al. (1993), examined general physical and psychosocial health ten years after the original study, when the children were 16 or 17 years of age. They found that children diagnosed as having DAMP at seven years of age continue to show health problems at 16, over and above those of the general population. The DAMP group had more febrile seizures, more substance abuse, more accidents, longer visual reaction times and a higher rate of gross and fine motor problems. However, although group data showed a higher proportion of problems in the DAMP group, a number of individuals in the group did relatively well. The authors comment that these results indicate that DAMP is a neurodevelopmental disorder with changing clinical

landmarks, which in some cases continues to cause difficulties throughout childhood and adolescence. They present this data in support for the
proposition that motor problems persist throughout childhood and argue
against the notion that children will grow out of it. Michaelson and
Lindhal (1993) reached a similar conclusion that, even if some children
do improve with age, there is still a large number whose motor problems
continue well beyond childhood.

Sugden and Wright (1998) note that it has sometimes been suggested
that a distinction can be made between children whose early motor problems are a relatively isolated phenomenon and children whose difficulties
are more extensive. The long-term prognosis for the former group is
thought to be much better. Bax and Whitmore (1987), for example, noted
that the intelligent *clumsy* children they identified at five years of age had
fewer problems at seven and ten years of age than children whose other
learning difficulties were already evident at five. However, Losse et al.
(1991) maintain that a distinction between isolated clumsiness and clumsiness with other difficulties is too simplistic. The main difference
between the Losse study and those of Bax and Whitmore (1987) and
Gillberg and Gillberg (1989) is that the Losse study extends well into the
secondary school years. Results from the study show that minor motor difficulties in early childhood should not be ignored. The effects of being
clumsy are evident into the teenage years and manifest themselves not
only in the motor domain but also in other areas.

These longitudinal studies which examine a number of developmental
variables provide invaluable descriptions of children with difficulties over
long periods of time, allowing researchers to examine mediating variables
that influence the individual's development and, in addition, they place
motor attributes in the context of other developmental areas and allow
complex interactions across different attributions to be examined. As
noted by Sugden and Wright (1998), if only motor variables had been
measured in the DAMP studies, the information that we now have concerning difficulties that seemingly disappear but re-emerge in other areas
would have been lost.

The results of the studies concerned with long-term prognosis of DCD
are still somewhat equivocal although, as noted by Sugden and Wright
(1998), there is a clearer picture developing as research in the area
becomes tighter and re-examines previous work. What is evident is that
there are children who do not spontaneously grow out of the condition
and there are children who literally suffer from the effects of DCD for considerable periods of their childhood. The long-term prognosis of DCD is
an important question for research to answer but, even if DCD is a temporary difficulty for some children, the anxiety felt by the children and the
poor motor skills exhibited are crucial issues to be dealt with at any time.

Associated difficulties and comorbid difficulties

Associated difficulties

The features associated with DCD are many and are not confined to the more noticeable motor skills. Various studies have identified a number of associated problems including underachievement at school (Henderson et al., 1989), lack of concentration (Lyytinen and Ahonen, 1989), behaviour problems (Gillberg and Gillberg, 1989; Losse et al., 1991), low self-esteem (Schoemaker and Kalverboer, 1994), poor social competence (Knight et al., 1992) and lack of physical hobbies (Cantell et al., 1994; Hall, 1988) – all of which can combine to detract from the child's academic progress.

In both DSM IV and ICD 10 there is mention of associated behaviours that accompany DCD, with difficulties in academic achievement, behaviour, self-concept, poor motivation and attention being some of the most commonly noted. Losse et al. (1991) found that there was a higher incidence of low academic achievement, poor behaviour and self-concept problems in children with DCD than in a control group. In other studies the higher incidence of associated behaviours is often quoted and it does raise some fundamental issues ranging from the pragmatic viewpoint of how one sets priorities for intervention to the more fundamental question surrounding the validity of separate syndromes in developmental disorders.

Many studies bear witness to the varied problems displayed by children with DCD. Gubbay (1975a) found that children were rejected by their classmates; Keogh and colleagues (1979) found that children with DCD attempted to cover up their difficulties by exhibiting disruptive behaviours in class. Kalverboer (1988) found that children with DCD were also considered to be withdrawn, submissive, and self-conscious, while Henderson et al. (1989) showed that children with movement difficulties were unrealistic in the way they set goals for themselves, had lower self-esteem and were less inclined to accept responsibility for what might happen to them.

Although, as pointed out by Sugden and Henderson (1994), bright and well adjusted *clumsy* children do exist, they are in the minority; it is far more common to find children whose poor movement skills are accompanied by educational or behavioural problems.

> Although a causal relationship has not been clearly established between DCD and school achievement, there is good evidence to suggest that there is a strong correlation. (Sugden and Henderson, 1994)

Sometimes the fact that children with movement difficulties do less well academically than would be expected from their cognitive ability can be directly explained by problems with handwriting, poor presentation, slowness to complete work and disorganization. At other times, low self-esteem, difficulties in concentrating, unhappiness because of bullying or rejection, will ultimately mean that these children will fail to show their true potential in the classroom. A study carried out by Schoemaker and Kalverboer (1994) found some children whose lack of competence in the motor domain contrasts sharply with their academic and social success. However, far more common are those whose movement difficulties are accompanied by lack of confidence, poor motivation, low self-esteem, depression, and social isolation. In a study by Smyth and Anderson (2000), it was found that, as a group, children with coordination disorders spent longer alone in the school playground, more time watching other children play, and at some ages spent more time moving around the playground without being engaged in any game or structured activity. In agreement with Schoemaker and Kalverboer (1994), Smyth and Anderson (2000) suggest that exclusion or withdrawal is already operating and some children with coordination problems are isolated from social play by the age of six years.

It is often assumed that the emotional problems experienced by children with DCD are simply a secondary consequence of their movement difficulty. However, Sugden and Henderson (1994) suggest that a more useful way of understanding the relationship is to view them as being in continuous interaction with each other. It is easy to see how being poorly coordinated from an early age can have negative effects; even at a very early age social rejection by peers may occur as the child with DCD is seen as an unpopular playmate. Such rejection marks the beginning of a cycle of lack of participation, reluctance to learn new skills, resistance to practice, declining confidence, lack of self-esteem and social isolation. 'If such a cycle is not broken, then the consequences for some teenagers can be severe' (Sugden and Henderson, 1994).

Comorbid difficulties

Children with Developmental Coordination Disorder (DCD) are part of a larger group which has come to be termed *developmental disabilities*. Children described in this way include those with specific difficulties in the areas of attention, language, literacy, social skills and motor coordination, and are often described by such terms as Developmental Dyslexia, Attention Deficit/Hyperactivity Disorder (ADHD), Autistic Spectrum Disorder (ASD), Specific Language Impairment (SLI) and Developmental Coordination Disorder (DCD). Developmental dyslexia includes specific difficulties in the area of reading and writing. Attention Deficit/Hyperactivity Disorder involves a persistent pattern of inattention and/or hyperactivity/impulsivity and occurs in academic or social situations. The

Autistic Spectrum Disorder includes both ASD and Asperger's Syndrome with impairment of social interaction, communication and a restricted repertoire of behaviours being common characteristics.

The frequency of comorbidity among children with DCD has been examined by a number of researchers including Dewey et al. (2000, 2002), Gillberg (1998), Gillberg and Kadesjö (1998, 2000), Hill (2001), Kaplan et al. (1998, 2001), Kavale and Nye (1985–86), O'Hare and Khalid (2002) Silver and Hagin (1990), Sugden and Wann (1987) and Wilson and McKenzie (1998).

Dewey and colleagues (2002) investigated the overlap between DCD and problems in attention, learning and psychosocial adjustment and concluded that children with DCD frequently display other disorders of development; results indicated that all children with DCD are at risk for problems in learning, attention and psychosocial functioning. Similarly, Kaplan and colleagues (1998) investigated the overlap between reading (dyslexia), attention and motor deficits and found sufficient evidence to recommend that the common occurrence of at least two out of three of these problems should be considered the norm rather than the exception.

Hill (2001) conducted a review of the literature on SLI and reported a substantial comorbidity between SLI and poor motor skills and suggests that SLI is not, in fact, a specific disorder of language. Similar findings have been found by Gillberg and colleagues who have extensively examined the overlap of attention and motor problems, a condition they refer to as DAMP (deficits in attention, motor control and perception) (Gillberg and Rasmussen, 1982a; Gillberg et al., 1982; Kadesjö and Gillberg, 1999a, b). They found that approximately half of the seven-year-old children that had been diagnosed with DCD also had moderate to severe symptoms of ADHD. They also reported that DCD was associated with reading comprehension problems at 10 years of age. Figure 3.1 shows some of these disorders co-existing with DCD.

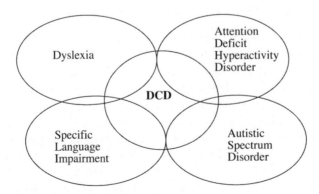

Figure 3.1 Comorbid conditions.

What is clear from the many research studies investigating comorbidi-ty, is that there is evidence indicating that DCD is not a uniform disorder. Rather, there appears to be a range of comorbid conditions of DCD, all requiring different treatment and all with different outcomes. Indeed, Dewey et al. (2002) state the results of their study indicate that

> all children with developmental movement problems, no matter what degree or severity, are at risk for problems in learning, attention and psy-chosocial functioning. (p. 914)

These studies all point to the importance of detailed assessments of chil-dren presenting with movement difficulties, not only in the motor area but also in the areas of attention and academic achievement.

Below is presented a brief overview of some of the developmental dis-orders which research studies have shown can co-exist with DCD.

Developmental Dyslexia

Developmental Dyslexia is a specific learning disability characterized by difficulties with accurate and/or fluent word recognition and by poor spelling abilities. These difficulties typically result from a deficit in the phonological component of language that is often unexpected in rela-tion to other cognitive abilities. Secondary consequences may include problems in reading comprehension and reduced reading experience that can impede growth of vocabulary and background knowledge which impedes academic achievement or daily living (Hulme and Snowling, 1997; Snowling, 2000). Characteristics of developmental dyslexia in the pre-school child may include delay or difficulty in devel-opment of clear speech and a tendency to jumble words and phrases over some time.

Attention-Deficit Hyperactivity Disorder (ADHD)

Attention-Deficit Hyperactivity Disorder is characterized by developmen-tally inappropriate impulsivity, attention, and in some cases, hyperactivity. ADHD is a neurological disorder that affects 3–5 per cent of school-age children (DSM IV, 1994; Barkley, 1998; Hinshaw, 1994). Although individuals with this disorder can be very successful in life, without identification and proper treatment, ADHD may have serious consequences including school failure, depression, conduct disorder, substance abuse and job failure. The disorder has been described by a variety of terms including Minimal Brain Dysfunction, Hyperkinetic Reaction of Childhood, and Attention-Deficit Disorder With or Without Hyperactivity. With the classification system of DSM IV and DSM IV TR

(1994 and 2000) the disorder has been renamed Attention Deficit Hyperactivity Disorder, reflecting the importance of the inattention characteristics of the disorder as well as hyperactivity and impulsivity.

Typically, ADHD symptoms arise in early childhood but some symptoms persist into adulthood and may pose life-long challenges. Although the official diagnostic criteria state that the onset of symptoms must occur before age seven, leading researchers in the field of ADHD argue that criterion should be broadened to include onset any time during childhood (Barkley, 1998). Criteria for three primary subtypes include failure to give close attention to details or making careless mistakes, difficulty sustaining attention, not appearing to listen, struggling to follow through instructions, difficulty with organization, avoiding or disliking tasks requiring sustained mental effort, is easily distracted and forgetful in daily activities. Additionally, children with hyperactivity also display fidgeting with hands or feet or squirming in chair, difficulty remaining seated, running about or climbing excessively, difficulty engaging in activities quietly, talking excessively and difficulty waiting or taking turns, interrupting or intruding upon others (DSM IV, 1994; Wender, 2000).

Autistic Spectrum Disorder (ASD)

Autistic Spectrum Disorder includes the conditions of Autism and Asperger's Syndrome. ASD is the most severe of the developmental disabilities with an incidence of approximately 1 per 1000 live births with a ratio of 3.5 males to 1 female affected. The primary difficulty in ASD is the way the brain processes and integrates information, resulting in problems of social interaction, communication and behaviour and, although ASD is a severely disabling condition, outcomes for children with ASD are improving as more effective interventions and more appropriate community resources are developed (Baron-Cohen et al., 1993; Bishop, 1999; Frith, 2003).

The primary characteristics of ASD include impaired reciprocal social interactions, impaired communication, and restricted behaviours. Communication and language problems are also primary in ASD (Gillberg and Coleman, 2000). Another primary characteristic is restricted range of behaviours, activities and interests. Lower functioning ADS children frequently engage in repetitive bodily movements, self-stimulatory behaviours and sometimes even self-abuse and their play patterns are restricted and repetitive. Those children displaying higher functioning may focus on some topics that are narrow and generally uninteresting to others: bus schedules, train timetables, geography or numbers (Bishop, 1999; Jordan, 1999).

Specific Language Impairment (SLI)

A recent epidemiological study of monolingual English-speaking kindergarten children in the United States found that approximately 8 per cent of boys and 6 per cent of girls have a significant developmental language impairment of unknown origin, referred to as specific language impairment (SLI; Tomblin et al., 1997). SLI is diagnosed in children who exhibit significant language deficits despite adequate educational opportunity and non-verbal intelligence. A diagnosis is often made after ruling out the presence of other constitutional disorders. Children with SLI differ in the degree to which they have problems articulating speech sounds, expressing themselves verbally and comprehending the speech of others. SLI has broadly been classified into three subtypes of articulation disorder, expressive language disorder and mixed expressive and receptive language disorder. However, it has been proposed that the variability in the profile of deficits may reflect variation in the severity of the underlying disorder.

Summary

Most of the work concerning the identification of children with DCD has concentrated upon school age children and how the disorder manifests itself through difficulties related both to daily living and to school related tasks. A number of studies have investigated the outcome of this disorder in adolescence, noting that appropriate intervention and management strategies play a crucial part in the successful resolution of the difficulty. Little work has been completed in the age range three to five years. This text examines children three to seven or eight years of age and the latter part of that range overlaps with the literature looking at five to seven year olds.

The outcomes of possessing low functioning motor skills, whether diagnosed as DCD or not are seen in poorly coordinated living skills, and those motor skills needed for progress in the formal and informal learning environment of school. Motor competency is an important determinant of a child's educational progress as well as more general development. In most cultures, for example, learning in the early years is based on exploratory play, which in turn involves movement. As the child gets older, the ability to write legibly and with adequate speed becomes a prerequisite for note-taking and examination performance as well as being a component of more general literacy skills. In addition, lack of movement skills may exclude a child from playground activities, leading to social isolation, loneliness, and even depression (Gillberg and Gillberg, 1989; Hellgren et al., 1993; Losse et al., 1991; Smyth and Anderson, 2000).

The long-term prognosis for these children, in general, is not good, although some children do catch up with their peers (Cantell et al., 1994; Geuze and Börger, 1993; Losse et al., 1991; Lyytinen and Ahonen, 1989). The evidence thus far shows that those children who receive help will make gains in their motor skills and associated behaviours (Polatajko et al., 1995b; Sims et al., 1996a; 1996b; Sugden and Chambers, 2003; Wright and Sugden, 1998). In view of this, it is crucial that young children with movement difficulties are consistently identified and assessed in order that the nature of their difficulties can be determined and, where necessary, appropriate management of the disorder may ensue.

CHAPTER 4

Assessing young children with movement difficulties

Introduction

In the first three chapters it has been noted that movement is a fundamental component of human life with the ability to make precise controlled movements being so much part of daily living. The conduct of countless acts becomes so automatic that they scarcely intrude upon consciousness and, as such, we often forget their diversity, richness and functional importance. It is hoped that by the time children reach school age they have built up a repertoire of skills that enable them to function effectively in the classroom and playground. However, some children arrive at school lacking in the skills necessary for them to cope with the demands of the school environment. For some, this could be a direct result of lack of experience, while for others it could be a more complex problem with potential long-term consequences (Cantell et al., 1994; Losse et al., 1991).

The overall picture of children with DCD shows that the basic fundamental skills of sitting, standing, walking, running, reaching and grasping emerge even though they may be delayed. However, although these skills may be performed at a rudimentary level, the necessary development to competent functional skills has not occurred (Henderson, 1992; Keogh and Sugden, 1985; Sugden and Henderson, 1994). This lack of development means that, by comparison, children with DCD fall behind their peers in some or all of these functional skills, resulting in a detrimental effect on their progress in school and in the activities of daily living.

The period from two to seven years of age is generally recognized as a time of acquisition of a number of fundamental motor skills leading to the development of a large repertoire of movement skills (Keogh and Sugden, 1985). If the fundamental skills are not developed in these years, problems may occur later and consequently on entry into school the child with DCD may not have mastered the skills necessary for them to participate fully in classroom and playground activities. In addition there is evidence that poor motor development may affect other areas of school activity including underachievement at school (Henderson et al., 1989), lack of concentration (Lyytinen and Ahonen, 1989), behaviour problems (Gillberg and Gillberg, 1989; Losse et al., 1991), low self-esteem (Schoemaker and Kalverboer, 1994), poor social competence (Knight et al., 1992) and lack of physical hobbies (Cantell et al., 1994; Hall, 1988).

We have also noted in Chapter 3 that the long-term prognosis for children with DCD who do not receive help in general is not good (Cantell et al., 1994; Losse et al., 1991). This is particularly true if specific intervention is not given (Polatajko et al., 1995b; Sims et al., 1996a; Wright and Sugden, 1998). When intervention is given the results are encouraging (Polatajko et al., 1995b; Polatajko et al., 2001a; Sugden and Chambers, 1998; Wright and Sugden, 1998) but for intervention to be effective, children need to be *accurately and consistently identified and assessed*.

Uses and types of assessment

There are a number of uses and types of assessment. One large differentiation is between those instruments that are used in a formal testing situation and those that can be used flexibly by teachers/parents/carers as part of everyday activities. Both of these are in keeping with the American Psychiatric Association's DSM-IV (1994), which states that in order for a diagnosis of Developmental Coordination Disorder to be made a child must experience movement problems that are significantly below their peers and which significantly interfere with academic success or activities of daily living. However, the diagnosis cannot be made if the disturbance is due to a medical condition such as cerebral palsy or muscular dystrophy. If a child has mental retardation, the diagnosis of Developmental Coordination Disorder can only be made if the movement difficulties are in excess of those usually associated with mental retardation.

Diagnostic criteria for 315.4 Developmental Coordination Disorder

A. Performance in daily activities that require motor coordination is substantially below that expected given the person's chronological age and measured intelligence. This may be manifested by marked delays in achieving motor milestones (e.g. walking, crawling, sitting), dropping things, 'clumsiness', poor performance in sports, or poor handwriting.

B. The disturbance in Criterion A significantly interferes with academic achievement or activities of daily living. (DSM IV, 1994, pp. 54–5)

Early identification of children with DCD is important for a number of reasons. First, recognizing that a child has motor difficulties opens the way for providing support for the child and parents and provides strategies of how to cope with these difficulties. Secondly, early identification and subsequent intervention might prevent children with DCD from becoming discouraged about both academic and playground activities at an early age. This, in turn, might prevent the development of concomitant problems such as psychosocial problems (Schoemaker and Kalverboer, 1994; Skinner and Piek, 2001).

It is acknowledged that methods of identification and assessment are inextricably linked to the nature and characteristics of any disorder and, indeed, often determine the central features (Sugden and Wright, 1998). A major question when examining assessment processes and instruments is why the test is being employed and for what purpose will the results be used? Very often the questions run in tandem with who is using the test. At a fundamental level, one can regard some assessment regimes as being purely for screening purposes so that a large population can be reduced to a smaller sample identified as being at some kind of risk. Motor behaviour is frequently assessed as part of a larger battery of overall development and gives a professional an overview of a child's profile of abilities. Examples of tests such as these include the Bayley Scales of Infant Development (Bayley, 1993) and Griffiths Mental Development Scales for testing babies and young children from birth to eight years of age (Griffiths, 1967). However, Sugden and Wright (1998) point out that for a more detailed examination of motor behaviour, tests which directly address motor aspects of a child's functioning are required.

Henderson (1987) undertook a critical analysis of types of assessment instruments and methodology and in her review of assessment types, she divides tests into those which she labels traditional and have formed the basis of assessment by psychologists, paediatricians, therapists and teachers, and those she labels as alternative and have emerged as a result of the criticisms aimed at the traditional approaches. Henderson divides the traditional approaches into descriptive tests, diagnostic tests and neurodevelopmental test batteries. Descriptive tests are usually aimed at assessing functional performance in everyday activities, producing a quantitative measure of the child's performance. These tests use chronological age as the measure against which performance is judged and composite scores are used in a normative manner to compare child against child. Age-related measures for assessment are commonly utilized and indeed are presented here but, because of variability with any age, they must be treated with caution.

Jongmans (in Sugden and Chambers, 2005) asks an interesting question: what is meant by 'early' in the context of identification? Does this mean from the first moment that functional problems arise? Or does 'early' mean that the aim should be to identify children with motor problems even before they start to affect a child's daily functioning? Nowadays, identifying children with movement difficulties from the moment their difficulties are apparent is regarded as the minimum standard of service provision. Given the impact of movement difficulties on the academic achievement and daily lives of children, identifying these children even before their lives are significantly affected would be ideal but is not yet common practice and is potentially difficult.

Examples of current assessment instruments in the early years

Tests of motor behaviour in the early years are usually part of assessment instruments that evaluate overall ability. An example of this is the Bayley Scales of Infant Development (Second Edition) (BSID-II) (Bayley, 1993) updated in 1993. As with the previous edition, the BSID-II consists of a criterion – and norm – referenced test composed of three scales: the Mental Scale (178 items), the Motor Scale (111 items) and the Behavior Rating Scale (30 items). The Mental Scale assesses sensory-perceptual acuity, discriminations, and the ability to respond to these; object constancy and memory; learning and problem solving; and verbal ability, generalization, and classification while the Motor Scale focuses on body control and fine and gross motor skills which yields a standardized Psychomotor Development Index and an estimated developmental age. The Behavior Rating Scale (formerly called the Infant Behavior Record) assesses attitude, interest, emotion, energy, activity, and response to stimuli.

The stated uses of the Bayley Scales of Infant Development are to: identify children with developmental delays; design intervention programmes; to monitor the effectiveness of intervention programmes, as a tool for teaching parents about their infants development and as a research tool. Changes from the previous BSID version include an extended age range from one month to 42 months (previously 15 months) of age with new items applying to the expanded range; a redesign of stimulus materials with colour added; updated normative data; data collected on children with high-incidence clinical diagnoses (Down syndrome, prematurity, prenatal drug exposure).

Burton and Miller (1998) note that the original version of the BSID (1969), designed for depth and thoroughness, came to be considered by many scholars and practitioners the premier early movement skill assessment instrument. They further note that in the USA the BSID has been the most common standard used to establish the validity of other tests of early movement milestones; a fact, they state, that confirms the status of the test.

Another example is the Griffiths Mental Development Scales (Griffiths, 1967) which measures the rate of development of infants and young children from birth to eight years of age. It purports to measure trends of development that are significant for intelligence, or indicative of mental growth in babies and young children. There are two sets of Scales; one for each of the two age groups, 0–2 years and 2–8 years with 27 test items in the younger age group set and 22 in the older age group set. Record books or forms are used for scoring the scales. The Scales were standardized on a minimum of 20 subjects in each month of life from two weeks onwards and the descriptions of the methods employed are given in the books, *The Abilities of Babies* and *The Abilities of Young Children*, written by the author of the Scales. Descriptions are also given of frequency distributions and general validity of the Scales. In 1996, a major revision of the Griffiths 0–2 Scale was undertaken. The revision team carried out a complete restandardization of the Scale, adding eight new items to the apparatus and introducing a revised Record Form.

Construct validity was explored in a study by Luiz et al. (2001). A sample of 430 South African children from four ethnic groups (i.e. White, Mixed Race, Asian and Black) participated. The correlation coefficients obtained for the South African groups were compared with those Griffiths obtained in her work with the British standardization sample of the Griffiths Scales. The pattern of correlation for South African and British subjects was found to be similar. This suggests that the Scales are measuring a construct which is consistent across cultures and through time.

A study by Bowen and Colleagues (1996) examined the predictive value of the Griffiths assessment in extremely low birthweight infants. The objective was to assess the relationship between the Griffiths Mental Development Scales at one and three years and the Stanford-Binet Intelligence Scale and the Beery Test of Visual-Motor Integration at five years in extremely low birthweight children. Forty-five extremely low birthweight infants, without severe neurosensory impairment and who were cared for in a neonatal intensive care unit participated in the study. Results indicated that the three-year Griffiths GQ is a good predictor of the five-year Stanford-Binet Intelligence Scale for extremely low birthweight children and the authors put forward the suggestion that the Griffiths Mental Development Scale can be used to identify children who may benefit from intervention prior to school entry.

Specific motor assessment procedures

The two tests described above are general instruments of overall development. The aim in this chapter is to describe the development of an instrument that specifically addresses motor behaviour.

Context and assessment

A fairly recent strategy to detect children with DCD is to involve parents actively in providing clinical descriptions of their child and a recognition that to successfully intervene, any programme ought to be part of a child's daily life of which the family is a crucial part. This follows remarks of parents that they feel their concerns are often ignored while later on their worries were confirmed (Stephenson et al., 1991). School teachers are also actively involved in the child's daily life and, as such, are in a position to offer support and effectively put into practice strategies which will enable children to improve their motor skills in a familiar context, ensuring that any programme is part of the child's daily routine. Parental involvement may consist of asking them to provide appraisals of their child's motor functioning including concerns, estimations and predictions. It appears that, provided parents are properly guided by professionals and high-quality screening instruments, they can provide valuable insights and observations of their child (Glascoe, 2001). It is crucial to involve parents in the identification phase of children with DCD since they are often the only people who can provide enough detail of the way the motor problems of the child interfere with activities of daily living (Miyahara and Möbs, 1995).

The most recent conceptual model of the International Classification of Functioning, Disability and Health (ICF: WHO, 2001) appears to have influenced the way children with DCD are assessed and managed. This model describes the consequences of diseases or conditions for daily functioning at three interrelated levels: (1) structure and function; (2) activities; and (3) participation. The model also includes the influence of personal and external factors on these levels. Interactions between all components of the model determine for each individual child the current functional status. The idea that assessment instruments should reflect a child's activities in everyday life has been widely accepted for some time (Haley et al., 1992). This has prompted the use of instruments aimed at measuring the actual ability of the child to perform necessary daily activities during the identification process.

The importance of including functional assessments in a standard assessment battery for children with movement difficulties lies in the information it provides in determining intervention goals relevant for daily functioning. Such an approach toward management means that children are encouraged to find solutions to the motor problems they themselves want to solve without prescribing the exact way in which they should do so. In this way it is possible to fulfil the wishes of children to learn certain activities (e.g. cycling or writing). This should make it easier for them to participate in activities of daily living appropriate for their age.

Performance inadequacies on movement assessment tests will provide an initial indication of movement skill problems, but detailed and systematic observations of children with movement problems are also needed to fully identify the nature of a child's problems. The inability to perform a movement adequately is a general indication of movement difficulties; how a child attempts a movement can provide further insight into the problems that a child has.

Underlying principles

It is emphasized that assessment and intervention are inextricably linked with assessment being a critical part of the whole process and this process follows a number of guiding principles. First, it has been noted that a system of assessment and identification of movement skill problems needs to be based firmly on the developmental progression of children, the interaction with the task to be completed and the context in which it is being performed (see Figure 4.1). Secondly, the identification of children with movement problems should involve an assessment of movement performance in relation to some general expectations of what is adequate movement skill (Chapter 1). Thirdly, a principle guiding the work is that activities within the movement skill domain should be organized into a framework so that a class of activities can be identified, with remediation aimed at that class (Chapter 1). Fourthly, it is based on the specific difficulty a child is experiencing (Chapter 3). Finally, there is a wish to produce a test that can be used in school or at home to assess every day functional tasks. Our answer to this is to produce the Early Years Movement Skills Checklist (EYMSC) (see Figure 4.1 and Figure A2.1 (Appendix 2)). It is an instrument to be used by those closest to the child; parents and teachers. It is a functional test used in context and it is aimed to provide areas for intervention.

Development of the Early Years Movement Skills Checklist

Rationale and development

Despite a renewed interest in children with movement problems during the last 15–20 years, there has been to date a limited number of assessment instruments available to enable primary and early years school teachers to approach this area within the context of the daily routine of the school environment. There are some instruments available which assess motor behaviour as part of a larger battery of overall development,

EARLY YEARS MOVEMENT SKILLS CHECKLIST

Name .... Gender .... Date of birth ....

School ....…... Age ....y .... m

Assessed by .... Date of Test .... Class ....

Section 1	Section 2	Section 3	Section 4	Total	

Can Do		Cannot Do	
Well	Just	Almost	Not Close
1	2	3	4

SECTION 1 Self Help Skills

The child can

- Put on a T-shirt without assistance ....
- Take off a T-shirt without assistance ....
- Fasten accessible coat buttons ....
- Unfasten accessible coat buttons ....
- Feed self using fork and spoon ....
- Wash and dry hands ....

Section 1 Total ....

SECTION 2 Desk Skills

The child can

- Copy a circle and a cross from a completed example ....
- Pick up and place pieces in an interlocking jigsaw ....
- Turn single pages of a book ....
- Use scissors to cut across a piece of paper (e.g. 4" strip) ....
- Construct simple models using duplo, lego, megablocks ....

Section 2 Total ....

SECTION 3 General Classroom Skills

The child can

- Sit on the floor with legs crossed and back straight ....
- Carry books and toys across the classroom in order to put away ....
- Move around the classroom/school avoiding collision with stationary people/objects ....
- Move around the classroom/school avoiding collision with moving people/objects ....
- Move forward, backward, sideways, under and over when shown ....

Section 3 Total ....

Figure 4.1 Early Years Movement Skills Checklist.

SECTION 4 Recreational/Playground Skills

The child can

- Use fixed playground equipment (e.g. climbing frame, slide)   ....
- Ride a variety of moving vehicles (e.g. pedal car, tricycle)   ....
- Kick a large stationary ball   ....
- Throw a large ball overarm using both hands   ....
- Join in playground activities, demonstrating running and jumping   ....
- Walk on tip toes for 4 steps   ....
- Catch a large (10") ball with two hands   ....

Section 4 Total   ....

Figure 4.1 Early Years Movement Skills Checklist (contd).

such as the two previously described. However, for a more detailed examination of motor behaviour, tests which directly address motor development aspects of a child's functioning are required. There are also a small number of tests which assess motor behaviour in its own right, for example, the Movement Assessment Battery for Children (Movement ABC) (Henderson and Sugden, 1992); however, as yet, these tests do not specifically focus on very young children.

As the focus is on the movement skill problems children may experience within their everyday situation, it is important that the assessment instrument can be used flexibly by teachers/parents/carers as part of everyday activities, and not within an artificially created testing situation. The issue is how they perform on a day-to-day basis and not on a one-off specific motor skill or task. This is in keeping with the American Psychiatric Association's DSM-IV (1994) and DSM-IV-TR (2000) which states that part of a diagnosis of Developmental Coordination Disorder involves a child experiencing movement problems which significantly interfere with academic success or activities of daily living.

Performance measures on movement assessment tests provide an initial indication of movement skill problems, but detailed and systematic observations of children with movement problems are also needed to fully identify the nature of a child's problems. The inability to perform a movement adequately is a general indication of movement difficulties; how a child attempts a movement can provide further insight into the problems that a child has. An additional consideration in measuring movement problems is movement-related behaviours which are important when moving and participating in movement activities (Keogh et al., 1979). Movement-related behaviours are important to consider as they may influence the child's achievements in the motor domain and, as such, add to the overall profile of the child's abilities.

The Checklist (The Early Years Movement Skills Checklist) includes items which are age-appropriate and is an instrument designed to be used flexibly by teachers or parents to describe more accurately the difficulties some children are experiencing in the motor area. It provides some detail about an individual child's performance with respect to functional competence in realistic everyday situations. The Checklist is based on the theoretical framework that recognizes that an individual always performs a task in a contextual setting. By constructing the Checklist in this way it is possible to use the profile of a child's score in a diagnostic manner to address specific concerns that the Checklist highlights. For example, a child's performance may be seen to be weighted in one of the areas only, thus pointing to the specific area of need. This will then give specific guidelines for intervention.

The *content* of assessment and identification of movement skill problems is based firmly on the developmental progression of children, the interaction with the task to be completed and the context in which it is being performed (Chapter 1).

The identification of children with movement problems involves an assessment of movement performance in relation to some general expectations of what is adequate movement skill. Tasks have been included because they are demanded of the child in the early years environment. The focus of interest is how a child performs a task on a daily basis and, therefore, the Checklist contains items which can be observed by teachers/parents as part of the child's daily routine.

The *organization* of the Early Years Movement Skills Checklist is split into sections. When assessing a child, the starting point is often a list of activities on which the child is failing. This is useful in that it allows the range and extent of the child's difficulties to be considered. However, this does leave the teacher or therapist with the problem of helping with every single task the child finds difficult. It is necessary to go beyond this preliminary analysis to an approach which organizes and classifies the tasks into a *framework* linked to effective intervention. The categorization of functional skills by Keogh and Sugden (1985) was taken as a starting point in the development of a framework for the Early Years Movement Skills Checklist. This classification involves categorizing movement according to mover-environment relationships, using a framework first proposed by Gentile and colleagues (1975). The framework involves four sections: Child stationary – Environment stable, Child moving – Environment stable, Child stationary – Environment changing, Child moving – Environment changing. The starting point for the framework is a recognition that an individual performs a task in a contextual setting. Thus, when a task is being performed, an examination of both the individual and the state of the environment is required. The individual performs movements either with the body stationary or movements which involve the body moving. In addition, some movements involve limb manipulation and in this situation the body can be either stationary or moving. Similarly, the environment can be either stable or unstable. It is important, therefore, to analyse movement in each of these contexts. This type of analysis relates to the child's difficulties in such a way that distinctions can be drawn between those occasions when a child is in control of their own actions in a stable environment and those occasions when the child must respond to the demands of a moving environment.

Although this was an attractive proposition and, indeed, follows that format of the Movement ABC Checklist (Henderson and Sugden, 1992), after consultation with early years educators, it was felt that these four categories were far too complex for young children, and the activities within them would be beyond their experience. Therefore, alternative ways in which to categorize the activities were considered.

The motor component

Establishment of vocabulary of functional movement skills

After noting the general content and organization of the Checklist, the primary function of the Checklist was addressed; the core motor component of coordination disorders. Initially, the following sources were used in order to generate a list of functional activities seen in three- to five-year-old children (List 1): Cohen and Volkmar (1997), Cratty (1986), Espenschade and Eckert (1967), Gallahue (1982), Goldfield (1995), Griffiths (1967), Haywood (1993), Kalverboer et al. (1993), Keogh and Sugden (1985), Klin et al., (1997), Knobloch and Pasamanick (1974), Koegel and Koegel (1996), Prizant et al., (1997), Schmidt (1991), Schuler et al. (1997), and Wetherby et al. (1997). The activities in this list are derived from the movement skills typically seen in early years classes and those which are well within the developmental boundaries of three- to five-year-old children: body control such as that seen in walking, running, jumping, hopping, throwing and balancing; manual control such as self-help skills including dressing, washing and feeding, construction skills, holding grips for writing and drawing, and bimanual control; and control of limb movements.

Construction and categorization of the Checklist

At every stage of the construction of the Checklist, professionals involved with young children were consulted as to the appropriateness and suitability of the proposed activities. The professionals included paediatric physiotherapists, paediatric occupational therapists, health visitors, speech therapists, nursery headteachers, nursery teachers and university lecturers and researchers. The focus of the interviews with the professionals centred on the following aspects: the appropriateness of the activities contained in the Checklist, the degree to which the activities are functional and everyday skills, the specific nature of the activities, suggestions of further activities to include in the Checklist and the categorization of the activities into a framework. In the light of the comments made by the professionals consulted, appropriate modifications were made at various stages of the construction of the Checklist.

Other versions were constructed using some of the items contained in the original list of activities and some of the items suggested by the professionals consulted. They were constructed by working bottom up from the list of activities and considering the appropriateness of each item in relation to the developmental literature and in relation to the comments made by the professionals who were consulted as to the appropriateness of the activities.

At the same time, an ecological psychology perspective was employed, recognizing the importance of functional skills in context with the environment affording certain actions (top down: this approach is elaborated in Chapter 5). This was done by determining the type of skills which are seen in the school environment and considering the appropriateness of them in relation to the specific age group. This was then combined with the list of activities mentioned above.

By working bottom up and top down the items from the list of activities fell naturally into four distinct categories: *Self-Help Skills*, *Desk Skills*, *General Classroom Skills* and *Recreational/Playground Skills*. Each of these categories includes four or five classes of items as indicated below.

Self-help skills

This section involves the child's capabilities in those activities of self-help that occur every day in a range of contexts.

Clothing

Items which will demonstrate the planning and motor control involved in putting on and taking off clothes.

Small fasteners

Items which demonstrate dexterity in bimanual control and fine motor control in fastening and unfastening.

Feeding/drinking

Items which demonstrate competence (bimanual control and coordination) in feeding oneself.

Washing etc.

Items which demonstrate competence in washing, involving bimanual control and repetitive movements.

Desk skills

Here the concern is primarily with activities at school.

Representation

Items which show competence in representation skills that is writing, drawing and copying involving planning and organization as well as manual control.

Small object manipulation

Items which show manual dexterity and control together with eye–hand coordination.

Page/paper manipulation

Items which demonstrate manual dexterity and eye–hand coordination with non-resistant materials such as paper.

Scissors, glue etc.

Items which demonstrate manual dexterity and control together with eye–hand coordination.

Constructing models

Items which demonstrate planning, manual dexterity and control together with eye–hand coordination.

General classroom skills

In early years' classes and nurseries, children move around a great deal and this section involves their competence in a variety of skills in the classroom.

Sitting appropriately

Items which demonstrate postural control and static balance.

Carrying

Items which demonstrate the motor control and planning involved in carrying objects around the classroom.

Moving around not bumping into people/objects

Items which demonstrate the motor control, planning and perception involved in avoiding collision with other people and objects when moving around.

Directional commands (forward, backward, imitation)

Items which demonstrate the motor control, coordination and planning in moving in various directions.

Recreational/playground skills

Both at school and at home, young children play and engage in recreational skills. This section looks at a range of these skills.

Use of playground equipment

Items which demonstrate competence in motor control, coordination and planning, together with static and dynamic balance.

Moving etc.

Items which demonstrate postural control, coordination, and planning together with dynamic balance.

Ball skills

Items which demonstrate motor control, eye–hand coordination together with static and dynamic balance.

Run/jump/hop etc.

Items which demonstrate competence in motor control, dynamic balance, coordination and planning.

Balance

Items which demonstrate postural control and static or dynamic balance.

Having decided on the categories for activities, each class of items was considered individually and various activities within each class were identified. The movements involved in each class were considered and then it was decided which activity would best represent this class of activity. These activities were taken from the original list of activities that was developed from the literature and the activities suggested by the professionals who were consulted. At the same time the appropriateness of the activity for the age group and the context in which it would occur was taken into account.

All of this leads to the selection of items, each of which represents a close knit group of activities. When developing the Checklist, for each item it was decided which functional every day activity were representative of the class of activity and the activities that are listed for each class of items are believed to best represent that particular class.

At this stage in the development of the Checklist, a scoring system was added. There are four alternative responses which describe how well the child deals with an activity. The four responses are divided into two categories *Can Do* and *Cannot Do*; the Can Do category is divided into two sections *Well* or *Just* and the Cannot Do category is divided into *Almost* and *Not Close*. The response to each activity is scored on a four-point scale from 1 (Well) to 4 (Not Close). Thus, a high score on the Checklist indicates that a child is not able to perform activities as well as a child with a low score. First, it is necessary to decide whether the child *can* or *cannot* do the task. Then, consider how well the child performs that particular task. If the child *can* do it, can they perform it *Well* or only *Just*? If the child *cannot* perform the task, can they *Almost* do it or are they *Not Close*? In this way, the child is rated on how he or she performs the task not on whether he or she is good or not so good for his or her age. Each item requires a single overall rating and scores for each section are then added and the result entered at the end of each section. These four separate totals are then entered in the summary box at the beginning of the Checklist and summed to achieve an overall rating.

Tasks are included in the Checklist because they are demanded of the child in the early years environment. The focus of interest is how a child performs a task on a daily basis and, therefore, the Checklist contains items which can be observed by teachers/parents as part of the child's daily routine. The Checklist provides some detail about an individual child's performance with respect to functional competencies in realistic everyday situations. Therefore, one of the aims of the Checklist is to obtain a measure of the child's typical patterns of functioning in familiar and representative environments, such as home and school. It will provide an essential indicator of the extent to which the child is able to utilize his or her potential in the process of adaptation to environmental demands.

An integral part of the construction of an assessment instrument is to determine to what extent the instrument identifies what it is meant to identify. In the case of the *Early Years Movement Skills Checklist* a study was carried out to determine whether the Checklist would distinguish between young children with movement difficulties and those without movement difficulties. A brief overview of the study is presented below but a detailed account can be found in Appendix 1 (see also Chambers, 2000; Chambers and Sugden, 2002).

The collection of data involved Checklists being completed by teachers in 34 randomly selected schools for 420 three- to five-year-old children. The schools randomly selected to participate in the study consisted of 24 nursery schools/classes, 25 reception classes, and 22 Year 1 classes and involved 71 class teachers. Each teacher was asked to choose three boys and three girls from their class, according to random numbers supplied with the instructions. In classes where there was more than one adult (for example, teaching assistant, nursery nurse, regular parent helper) one extra Checklist was left with the teacher to be completed by the other adult, independently of the teacher, in order to obtain a measure of inter-rater reliability. At the end of the three-week period, completed Checklists were collected from each of the schools. When returning to schools to collect the completed Early Years Movement Skills Checklists, one further Checklist was left with each class teacher, with the request that it was completed on one of the same children one month after the initial Checklist, as a measure of test–retest reliability.

In order to obtain a measure of the predictive validity of the Early Years Movement Skills Checklist, a sample from the four- and five-year-old children was selected for testing on an established test of motor skills. The selected sample included children whose scores were in the lowest 5 per cent of the total scores of the Checklist (Sample 1), those children whose scores were in the lowest 5–10 per cent of the total scores of the Checklist (Sample 2) and a random sample of 5 per cent of children whose scores were not in the bottom 10 per cent of the total scores of the Checklist (Sample 3). This was to establish whether children scoring poorly on the Early Years Movement Skills Checklist would also score poorly on an established test of motor skills and children who scored satisfactorily on the Early Years Movement Skills Checklist would also score satisfactorily on another measure of motor skills. The assessment instrument that was used to measure predictive validity was the test component of the Movement Assessment Battery for Children (Movement ABC) (Henderson and Sugden, 1992). The specificity and sensitivity index of the Checklist was also calculated.

Data analysis revealed that the Early Years Movement Skills Checklist identifies movement difficulties in the three to five years age group and significant differences were found between children who displayed movement difficulties and those who did not. The children identified as displaying movement difficulties were found to be a significantly different group from their well-coordinated peers. In addition, it shows developmental progression of children aged 3–5 years – overall scores for three-year-old children are higher (indicating poorer performance) than overall scores for the four-year-old children which, in turn, are higher than overall scores for the five-year-old children.

The overall interrater reliability correlation and the overall test–retest reliability correlation for the Checklist were both found to be good and results for both were highly significant. A validity study focusing on the predictive validity compared data collected from the Checklist with data from a normative motor skills test from the Movement ABC (Henderson and Sugden, 1992) and a significant correlation was found for the whole of the selected sample.

In conclusion, the study confirmed that the Early Years Movement Skills Checklist is able to distinguish between children with and without movement difficulties and is also able to distinguish between children whose difficulties encompass all areas of functioning and children whose difficulties may be apparent in one or two areas only. In addition, reliability data has demonstrated the interrater and test–retest reliability of the Checklist. Predictive validity confirmed the Checklist to be a valid identification instrument in terms of identifying children with movement difficulties and in terms of the sensitivity and specificity.

The Early Years Movement Skills Checklist, along with instructions for the administration and interpretation of it, are contained in Appendix 2.

CHAPTER 5

Intervention in the early years

Introduction

When examining ways of intervening with children in the early years, a number of variables guide the decisions that have to be made. This chapter attempts to detail these decisions, weighing up the pros and cons followed by guidelines that, hopefully, will help parents and professionals work with young children in a productive manner. The chapter is not a cookbook that can be slavishly followed as this would imply that there is a 'one size fits all' which is clearly not the case. It does, however, present practical advice and, together with some examples of programmes of activities, will enable parents, teachers and other professionals make intelligent decisions about working with young children in their charge. The chapter begins by examining the difficulties faced by children and some of the dilemmas that need to be resolved; it moves on to providing directions on how to obtain help, particularly through the Special Educational Needs Code of Practice (DfES, 2001). A further section promotes general guidelines for working with children whether at home or in school and, finally, there is a selection of practical examples provided to illustrate the type of activities that could be employed. These are not intended to be comprehensive and at the end of the chapter references are provided that are sources for further examples of practical activities.

What is the problem?

Concerns

In previous chapters, detail on children's motor development and motor impairment has been presented, laying the foundations for any intervention programme. The starting point for any programme is that someone is showing a concern about a child's development with this concern being predominantly in the motor area. This concern is shown by someone in close and fairly constant contact with the child, usually the parent, teacher, nursery nurse or childminder. At this point, it is useful to note that such conditions as cerebral palsy are usually picked up earlier than the general coordination difficulties referred to here and later known as Developmental Coordination Disorder (DCD).

Associated difficulties

It is rarely the case that a child will only show problems in the motor area, with difficulties often seen in language, cognition and social skills as part of a general concern for the overall development of the child. However, if a major factor is in the area of motor skills, it is usually of sufficient importance in the child's development for some kind of action to be taken. When observing a child, it is useful to make an evaluation of the influence the difficulty in motor skills is having on his/her overall daily functioning while recognizing that in many cases problems in this area are accompanied by other difficulties. This issue of associated difficulties or comorbid problems is one that will reappear throughout the chapter and is a factor influencing the line of approach to remediation that is being proposed. If, for example, a child has an attentional difficulty in addition to coordination problems, a line of approach would be to address the attentional difficulty first to ensure that any later remediation for the coordination difficulty is actually being attended to by the child. An alternative approach would be to utilize a task involving coordination as a motivator to aid in the attention process. The priority of one or the other of these options will vary with the child according to his/her profile.

Early intervention

Any concern for the development of a child naturally brings a worry to the parent and from a professional point of view to a teacher, health visitor or nursery nurse. This automatically leads to a desire to remediate the difficulty as quickly as possible. However, even though it is known that early intervention with any problem is usually beneficial, caution is advised about the line and intensity of any approach for a number of reasons. First, early identification of any difficulty can lead to fixed views about children and their difficulties and it is known that in many cases this is often incorrect. In Chapter 2 on motor development, it was shown that it is the multiple variables a child encounters in their lives that have an effect on their development and these can change. Thus, any view on the child should not be fixed and early identification should not become 'early prediction', leading to low and often false expectations from the child. Secondly, there are various reasons why a child may not be following the true normal course of development and the reason may not always reside within the child. A simple explanation, and one that is made much of in this chapter, is one of *opportunity of experience*; namely as a first step it is essential that the child has had chance to participate in the activities one normally sees in the developing two- to seven-year-old. *Thus, a fundamental principle is the one surrounding experience; that a child must be given the opportunity to engage in those motor activities normally experienced in the early years.*

Curriculum in the early years

The early years, as defined in the recent paper by the National Children's Bureau and Barnardo's (Anning, 2003), is from birth to seven years of age. Historically, there has been a division of responsibility in the UK between social services and education which has led to a plethora of types of placements in the early years, ranging from family centres, pre-school play groups, day nurseries, nursery schools, nursery and reception classes in primary schools. In the UK, it is probably true to say that compared with countries in Scandinavia and some other European countries, the provision has been haphazard and under-funded.

What to teach in the early years has been the subject of long debate but it is accepted that children learn in social groups that are set in cultural contexts. The curriculum is child-centred, based on a child's everyday experiences although 'curriculum' may not be the most appropriate word for the experiences of the under threes; it is possibly a little too formal. However, the DfES (2002) does refer to a framework that supports children's learning from birth to three noting four 'aspects' – *a Strong Child*; *a Skilful Communicator*; *a Competent Learner* and *a Healthy Child*.

Early childhood settings are characterized by *experiential learning based on practical and sensory-based learning which are embedded in everyday life*. Whether these are the developmentally appropriate practices, as they are labelled in the USA, or the similar models in Italy (Edwards et al., 1993) or the Te Wharika model in New Zealand (Ministry of Education, NZ, 1996), all look towards first-hand experiences in contexts, presented in themes and topic as the base. In the UK, Blenkin and Kelly (1997) reported that practitioners consistently rank social, emotional, physical and language as priorities together with the external pressure for cognitive outcomes to be prioritized. These practitioners from the different backgrounds of social services and education have combined to present a more cohesive offering in the early years. In most developed countries there is a policy of investing in the early years and promoting young children to become effective learners when they start formal schooling.

For three to five year olds, a curriculum model, Desirable Leaning Outcomes (DLO) was proposed and introduced in which three and four year olds were offered half a day of education in the areas of mathematics, knowledge and understanding of the world, personal, social and emotional, language and literacy, physical development and creative development. Although in some quarters this was seen as too formal too soon, much of these were incorporated in the Foundation Stage Curriculum for Under Fives (DfEE, 1999) and attainments are still a strong part of early years offerings. Thus, the setting in school for early intervention for children with movement difficulties is embedded in the educational context of the overall early years curriculum. For intervention at home, as will be noted, it should be firmly set in the everyday context of family life.

Low level experiential intervention

In all of the experiences, whether described as curriculum or desired learning outcomes, the physical domain is one that is prominent. As will later be described, it is often the case that difficulties in the physical domain at this stage of a child's life have a knock-on effect on other areas and, thus, intervention is seen as an important step forward.

In many cases, a child's difficulties can be traced to a lack of exposure to the full range of expected movement situations. A central theme that will appear throughout the chapter is one of '*low level experiential*' intervention with an emphasis on the children being presented with situations that engage them in the natural activities commensurate with their stage of development. In Chapter 2, there has been a description and explanation of these activities and how they develop. The approach is called 'experiential' and is also named 'low level'; this is not to assume that the intervention is anything but appropriate and proper but it is simply to emphasize that at this age the intervention should not go overboard and be intrusive, such that it becomes a chore. It should be geared to the needs of the child and, in most cases, low-level experiential intervention also indicates that at school the intervention takes place in the classroom alongside other children and only after a lack of success using this approach would a child be withdrawn from his or her peer group for special attention.

It is strongly advised that even in difficult cases intervention should take place, with appropriate help, in the normal classroom situation. In many cases, simple exposure with appropriate minimal instruction can be sufficient to put the child back on the track of normal development. This kind of intervention is more easily employed by parents and education and health professionals who come into contact with the child. There will be times when a child is showing more serious or pervasive difficulties and a structured approach to more direct teaching will be necessary. The point that is being emphasized links with the one made earlier about early intervention and the sensitivities surrounding it; namely that *any intervention should be at the appropriate level*. If it is too little, there is the possibility that the child simply engages passively in the activities and shows no improvement. On the other hand, if it is too much there is the danger of overly emphasizing the problem, thereby unnecessarily creating problems for the child and the family. A final recurring theme throughout the chapter is that *any intervention should fit into the daily life of the child and his/her context at school and at home*. There is much evidence available to show that unless an intervention programme fits into the daily life of the child, particularly with respect to family life, the chances of success are minimal (see, for example, Bernheimer and Keogh, 1995).

How to obtain help

Who to turn to: education and health

Parents often feel frustrated in trying to obtain help for their child who they believe has difficulties. The two obvious sources of help are from the health and education services and, in an ideal situation, professionals from both of these would work together to provide for the needs of the child.

When the child is below school age, that is s/he is two, three or four years of age, and the parent is worried, then the family's general practitioner or health visitor is often the first step. It is a good idea when visiting the doctor to have a list of very specific concerns about the child. This could include some of the activities the child is not doing which is believed s/he ought to be achieving, comparisons with other children and any behaviours the child has which ought to have gone away. After a consultation and a look at the child, the GP can, if necessary, refer to a paediatrician who is a specialist in child development or a child development centre. The paediatrician will examine the child and could perform what is called a neurological screening of the child. This involves the presentation of a number of tasks which have been especially selected to screen and identify movement and other difficulties. If the paediatrician believes there is a possibility of difficulties, s/he will refer the child to a paediatric occupational therapist or occasionally a physiotherapist for some form of management. In different heath authorities this can vary. The therapists are specialists in movement difficulties and should not only assist the child in therapy sessions but should also provide guidelines as to what parents can do on a daily basis at home.

The situation through the *educational system* is slightly different. A concern could arise through the parent and this concern can be conveyed to the nursery nurse or teacher. S/he will discuss the issue with the parent and suggest some form of intervention which can be done in the classroom or through a visiting professional such as a physiotherapist who, again, should provide activities for the parent and teacher to engage in. It could be the case that any difficulty is first raised by the nursery nurse/teacher who in consultation with the parent moves forward with some intervention programme.

It is important to note that there is an apparent paradox in what parents and professionals can do to help with respect to their own capabilities and situations. With parents and teachers it is clear that they have two major advantages when working with a child. First, and most importantly, they see the child on a daily basis and one of the major tenets of our recommendations is that whatever type of intervention is put in place it ought to follow the *principle of little and often*. That is, it is more beneficial for the child to engage regularly in activities for a short period of time rather than for one or two longer sessions over a protracted period.

There are two reasons for this; first, there is strong evidence from the motor control literature that this is the manner that learning best occurs and, secondly, it helps the child regard such activities as part of their daily life, something to be regularly engaged in and enjoyed. The second advantage teachers and, particularly, parents have is that they know the children well and have an obvious interest and concern for the children. However, parents and teachers are probably not specialists in this area and, thus, guidance for them is probably required. Specialists such as physiotherapists have the obvious advantage of knowledge and skill in the area but there is little opportunity to see the child on a regular basis or know the child in some detail.

One fact remains clear: that all other variables being equal, the greater the amount of appropriate practice in which a child engages, the more progress s/he is likely to make and the situation in which appropriate practice is maximized should be encouraged. Thus an ideal situation is for both parents and teachers and specialist professionals to work together and for teacher/nursery nurses and parents to be provided with the information from which they can enact any programme of intervention. They will then have the best of all worlds, with the knowledge and skills required to complete the task and the daily contact with the child which is so crucial. The role of professionals, such as physiotherapists, is crucial in this process; first by assessing the child and secondly by providing information for the teacher and parent to enact the programme. An aim of this chapter is to aid in this process and, hopefully, take the role of the physiotherapist by providing guidelines for assessment and intervention with the result being an empowering of both parents and teachers.

Special Educational Needs Code of Practice

When a child is at school age, procedures within the school situation in England and Wales are governed by a document called the *Special Educational Needs Code of Practice* (DfES, 2001). This section gives a brief overview of these procedures with a recognition that slightly different procedures may operate in other countries. In addition, although the procedures are specific to England and Wales, they do illustrate examples of good practice that are transferable to other countries if desired. The document gives practical guidance to all local education authorities and the governing bodies of maintained schools on their responsibilities to identify, assess and make provision for children with special educational needs (SEN).

The SEN Code of Practice stresses the importance of working with and taking into account the views of parents and pupils. It emphasizes the need for early identification and assessment of SEN and describes the conditions for the inclusion of pupils with SEN within mainstream schools.

> Partnership with parents plays a key role in promoting a culture of co-operation between parents, schools, LEAs and other. This is important in enabling children and young people with SEN to achieve their potential. (DfES, 2001, p. 16)

The SEN Code of Practice recommends the general adoption of a three-stage model of identification and assessment and sets out two-school based levels of intervention: *School Action* and *School Action Plus* in primary and secondary schools, and *Early Years Action* and *Early Years Action Plus* in early years settings. The Early Years Action and Early Years Action Plus stages, most pertinent to this text, are based in the schools and nurseries, and which will, as necessary, call upon the help of external specialists. The Code particularly emphasizes the importance of multi-agency approaches in meeting the needs of pupils. The third stage of identification and assessment involves the support of the LEA – in a very small number of cases the LEA will need to make a statutory assessment of special educational needs, possibly leading to a statement of special educational needs for a pupil. These stages are a means of helping schools and parents decide what provision is necessary and appropriate for a child. One child may have his needs met by Early Years Action, another may need to go to Early Years Action Plus while a third may need the intervention of the LEA.

The school/nursery based stages should make use of the parents' distinctive knowledge about their child and how s/he should be helped and the most effective provision is made when parents, schools and other professionals work in co-operation with each other. It is also essential that schools cooperate closely with other services, and for children with movement difficulties the health service is the most important. Very often a movement difficulty might have been identified by the child's general practitioner who should in turn notify the medical officer designated by the district health authority to work with the LEA on behalf of children with special educational needs.

School/nursery based stages which comprise the first two stages are seen as a continuous and systematic cycle of planning, action and review which the school puts into operation to cater for the child's needs, in this case improving his/her movement skills. It is a gradual extension of good practice, systematically introducing expertise when required.

Early Years Action

If a child is showing movement difficulties and there is concern by parents, the school or by another professional such as a general practitioner, paediatrician and other health personnel, this concern should be expressed to or raised by the class teacher/nursery nurse. It is of particular concern if a child is having difficulties despite receiving early education experiences. Although the emphasis here is on movement difficulties, it is known that at this age the difficulties are often of a more generic nature and it is useful to look at accompanying difficulties such as those in cognition, behaviour, language, or if the child shows consistent underachievement in comparison to peers. S/he in turn informs the head and SENCO and seeks advice if necessary. The teacher then gathers as much information about the child for an initial assessment on which to base special help within the normal classroom, such as breaking down tasks to make them easier and setting specific goals and targets to be monitored and recorded. An *Individual Education Plan (IEP)* can be devised at this stage which will include what the child can do well and areas that require assistance; suggestions for activities and ways of playing with the child for both parents and teachers, and a date to meet again to discuss progress. The SENCO is expected to take the lead in planning future interventions for the pupils in discussion with colleagues and parents, then monitoring and reviewing the action. If the child's progress is satisfactory and his/her movement skills appear to be improving, then the action at this stage may continue.

Early Years Action Plus

This stage is characterized by the involvement of external support services such as an Advisory Teacher for Pre School Children, who could, for example, provide advice on new IEPs and targets, more specialized assessments, advice on the use of new or specialist strategies or materials and, in some cases, provide support for particular activities. A decision to intervene at this level is made after a review of a child's progress or if parents, teachers or other professionals feel intensive action is necessary. The lead role for School Action Plus is taken by the school's SENCO who gathers all the available information from the school, parents and other agencies such as the health service professionals. This information is then used to draw up an *Individual Educational Plan (IEP)* for the child.

Individual Educational Plan

The Individual Education Plan (IEP) is a planning document identifying a pupil's immediate learning needs and the special arrangements, which need to be made to suit the individual pupil. It describes the arrangements made to monitor and review progress and ensure the pupil's entitlement is met. The IEP ensures that there are sufficient resources for a pupil's individual needs.

The IEP is monitored by assessing a pupil's progress against the targets. This means judging, reflecting and making decisions about how to proceed. It is a continuous process rather than a one-off activity. The purpose of this assessment process is to inform teachers and parents about the pupil and indicate what further action might be taken.

The SENCO should ensure close liaison between all teachers and the plan for a child with movement difficulties should contain the nature of the movement difficulties, provision to be made including support, targets and time limits, medical requirements, help from home, monitoring arrangements and review procedures. Above all, as part of a good assessment process the IEP will become an integral part of the child and family's school life. It is important for staff to communicate well with the child and family in order to make targets explicit and child friendly. It is important that both the child and parent know what it is they are working towards and feel clear about how they can achieve it.

An Individual Education Plan should clearly set out:

- the nature of the child's learning difficulties;
- action – the special educational provision – e.g. who is involved, what study programmes are being followed, how often extra help is given etc.;
- the parents' and teachers' part in all of this – what work is expected at home;
- what the school is trying to achieve and by when;
- any pastoral or medical needs;
- how progress is to be monitored and assessed;
- a date when this will be reviewed.

An IEP is evaluated a minimum of twice yearly involving all interested parties and if a child's progress is not satisfactory then the child should be considered for a *statutory assessment*.

Statutory assessment

The statutory assessment procedure involves professionals from a variety of disciplines assessing the child and providing information. In the case of a child with movement difficulties, the most relevant information will come from the parents, the school, educational psychologists and from medical and paramedical personnel such as paediatric occupational therapists and physiotherapists.

The LEA uses the above information to decide whether a statement of special educational need will be made. The main ground on which an LEA will base its decision is whether the child needs extra resources which are not normally available in mainstream schools in the area. If, for example, it is decided that a child with movement difficulties requires regular direct specialist teaching which could be a health input such as a paediatric occupational therapist, then a school could not be reasonably expected to

Table 5.1 Summary of the three-stage procedure in the Code of Practice

Early Years Action
• Initial concern by parent/teacher/other professional
• Teacher assesses child and action involves special help in normal class, or move to further stage, or no special education help required
• Progress reviewed

Early Years Action Plus
• Initial concern by teacher/parent/professional or from Early Years Action
• SENCO obtains help and information
• SENCO and teacher draw up IEP and implement it
• Review progress with child reverting to Early Years Action, continuing at Early Years Action Plus or moving to a statutory assessment

Statutory Assessment
• Headteacher requests statutory assessment
• Referral by child's school following 3 school procedures or from a formal request by a parent
• Multidisciplinary formal assessment by education, psychology, health, parental input and other services such as social services
• Statement of special educational need

make such provision within its own resources and a statement is necessary to fulfil this need.

The statement is the third stage of the three stages of identification, assessment and provision as laid down by the Code of Practice and it is usually the culmination of attempts at other stages to manage the child's difficulties and needs.

A fundamental part of this procedure is assessment; unless a child is accurately assessed noting strengths and weaknesses, the chances of success for any intervention programme is a lottery. The Early Years Movement Skills Checklist is presented in Chapter 4 (Figure 4.1) and Appendix 2 (Figure A2.1) and is an instrument that was developed because of a gap in the area; it is firmly based on research evidence and is relevant to both home and school situations. It is recommended that this is used with other forms of assessment.

Principles and general guidelines for intervention

Procedures have been outlined that can help a child receive the appropriate and specialist support from educational, health and psychological services. It is obvious that this type of support is paramount to the child's development and improvement. However, there are a number of activities parents and teachers/preschool professionals can do. They may not have the specialist background in the motor domain but they do have the twin advantages of knowing the child better than anyone else and seeing him/her on a very regular basis.

The following guidelines are prepared to help parents and teachers work with a child. They are not intended to be a substitute for specialist advice but a supplement to it. In an ideal world a child would be receiving specialist help from a therapist who, in turn, would be providing guidance for both teacher and parents so that they can work with the child on a daily basis. They have been developed from examining currently available programmes together with the intervention work we have been undertaking in Leeds over the last 10–12 years.

Table 5.2 provides an outline of the guidelines that are elaborated in the following pages. It is useful to present a summary of the points made in the following pages such that a quick reference can be made when working with a child.

Finally, we are looking to improve the child's motor coordination competence but this should not be an isolated aim; the *all round development* of the child should be our goal which includes competence, heightened self-esteem, an enthusiasm for physical activity.

Table 5.2 Summary of guidelines

I.   Accurately assess the child-leads directly to the type of activity to present (for detail see Chapter 4).

II. The more a child practises appropriately, the more improvement will take place particularly if the practice is 'little and often', that is 3–5 times a week of around half an hour duration.

III. Presenting tasks in a variety of ways leads to added competence when approaching a new situation.

IV. Making activities fun and meaningful will help the child look forward to them.

V.   Breaking tasks down into simpler components aids the learning of skills (analysing tasks).

VI. Changing the nature of any game by equipment, rules, object of the game etc. will aid the participation of children (adapting tasks).

VII. The help of a more competent other to provide support to the child by guiding, talking, generally assisting in the first instance and then slowly withdrawing, will move the child towards more independent learning (expert 'scaffolding').

VIII. Determine whether the child has a problem with understanding the task or performing the task (knowing and/or doing).

IX. From the child's profile of difficulties, assign priorities. Often the poor movement skill is heightened by inappropriate behaviour and changing these behaviours may have a beneficial effect all round.

X.   Give due consideration to the child's choices.

Accurate assessment to identify nature of the difficulty

This seems such an obvious thing to do and, yet, it is one that is rarely performed well. When a child is being assessed it is usually for two reasons. First, it is to confirm whether the suspected problem is real and, secondly, it is to specify exactly the nature of the difficulty leading to intervention. This second part is crucially important and once this is complete it could be argued that significant progress has been made with a view to helping the child. Detailed guidelines are presented in Chapter 4.

Accurate assessment of the difficulties and needs can be done in a number of ways and involves looking at the whole child and how s/he responds generally to situations not just his/her motor abilities. When observing the child, it is important to note *how* s/he performs, not just the end result. Obtaining detailed evidence over a period of a week or so helps build up a picture of the child's strengths and weaknesses in the motor area, together with how this affects them emotionally, whether their self concept is affected and what strategies they have tried in order to overcome these difficulties. Questions to be asked include 'Is the lack of competence in motor skills affecting other areas of the child's learning?' 'Is it affecting the child's interactions with other children?' 'Is it making them unhappy?' These observations are performed in the daily life of the child in everyday contexts.

Are other behaviours occurring as a result of the child's difficulties with movement? For young children the Early Years Movement Skill Checklist (EYMSC) (see above, Figure 4.1, Chapter 4) is used and for older ones the Movement Assessment Battery for Children (Henderson and Sugden, 1992). The objective is to gain as much detailed and specific evidence as possible concerning the child. The EYMSC is a checklist and the Movement ABC includes a checklist and a test to specify the nature of the difficulties. The ideal procedure is for the teacher in school plus the parent to use one of the Checklists to determine the nature of the difficulties, followed by the test being used by a professional such as an educational psychologist or a paediatric occupational therapist. The information gleaned from these can then be used to develop a management plan. Again, ideally it would be better if help is given by a professional who provides guidelines weekly or every two weeks which can be carried out in school or at home. In Chapter 4, there are more detailed guidelines for assessment.

Little and often

Little and often describes the amount and how often practice ought to take place. Thus, for a child who is showing problems in copying, writing and drawing, it is much better to give 15–20 minutes every day as opposed to 30–45 minutes' practice once or twice a week. From a motivational point of view, it is much easier to keep a child interested for a short time period than for a long one. Also, with short sessions the work becomes part of the child's daily routine, something the child expects to do every day. It is not something that brings instant success but is gained slowly and also surely over a period of time and becomes part of the child's and the parent/teacher's daily routine. This is particularly true if the parent is working in collaboration with a professional. From the child's assessment profile, itemize the tasks the child is finding particularly difficult. Take one of these tasks and others closely related and work with the child for about 15–20 minutes on each occasion. In a week, it is better to have three or four groups of tasks to work on so that the child does not become bored doing the same activity repeatedly. Each group of tasks should be chosen because the evidence gathered indicates that they present problems for the child.

Variety of practice

What kinds of tasks are given and how are they given? Let us say that the child has been assessed and that the main area of difficulty is in manipulation skills. They have problems with buttons, laces etc. The key to working in areas like this is to give lots of different types of tasks to practise in one particular area. In this case, one would give buttons of different sizes, laces, beads to thread, press studs, zippers, Velcro, snaps, pegs to move and others that are concerned with the child's manipulative skills. This is much better than concentrating on just one or two activities. First, it is much more motivating and, second, it allows the child to build up a large repertoire of skills which s/he can then bring to any situation. Similarly, with ball catching, use lots of different types of balls to catch, different throws, vary the distance and the type of throw, high, low, soft, or hard. More detail is presented on this later in the chapter.

The logic behind using variable practice lies in the concept of skill transfer or generalization. It is apparent that we are constantly required to transfer skills that are learned to different situations and contexts. Our lives present us with novel situations – the myriad of ways we can perform even simple tasks such as reaching and grasping places great demands on us. By using a variety of practices all in a 'class of events' rather than just one or two activities, we are ensuring that the learning is not just on one activity but is actually a solution to a variety of movement problems that are set by the environment.

One of the central themes of our work is that we employ variable practice on as many of the activities as possible. This lessens the disadvantage often aimed at task-oriented approaches that it has difficulty dealing with the transfer of skills. By taking the practice session away from direct individual tasks to groups of tasks linked by common demands on the child, there is a lessening of this problem.

Meaningful and enjoyable

When a child is practising a particular skill, there is more likelihood of success if the activity is enjoyable and meaningful to the child. This situation is not only more motivating for the child but, hopefully, it is what the child normally encounters in everyday life. Making games out of the practices, setting targets for some friendly self-competition, letting the child choose the activities, charting the results, are all ways in which tasks can be made more enjoyable. If throwing is involved, throw for targets; if it is a writing exercise let the child develop the story or make his/her own stencils; use cartoon figures rather than commercial sheets. All of these and many others make the activities fun and help the child look forward to them rather than view them as a chore to complete. Occasionally, let the child choose the level s/he wishes to perform at; it is possible to arrange tasks that do allow more than one level of difficulty. Encourage practice in a way that leads eventually to good performance in daily situations. Providing a clear structure gives them the stability they need to take command of the learning situation.

When the child has done well, it is important to give plenty of praise and let him/her know what the praise is for. For example: 'Well done, Amy, your writing is much better now that you are sitting correctly', which is much more appropriate than 'Good girl, Amy.' In the former, Amy knows what she has done and why, whereas in the latter she simply knows she is a good girl without knowing exactly for what reason.

Adapting and analysing tasks

When a child cannot perform a particular task there are two related actions that can be done. This first is to change or *adapt* the task so the child can participate or analyse and break the task down in order to learn it. A couple of examples may help to explain this. If a child cannot catch a ball thrown towards them a number of things can be done to help. The equipment can be changed, such as using a bigger ball, using one which has more 'feel' to it like a sponge ball and moves more slowly or using a bean bag. Here, the task is being *adapted* to make it easier for the child to participate.

A more complex example may involve adapting a whole game situation so that all children can be involved and participate. A game of softball may be changed so that the child hits the ball off a stationary cone rather than have it thrown towards them. The fielders then may have to pick up the ball, make two passes before placing the ball back on top of the cone before the hitter returns to base. Many examples of this type can be derived in numerous situations.

Examples of adaptation include:

Equipment

- size of ball
- weight of ball
- height of net
- width of goal
- size of bat
- stationary/non-stationary ball contact

Rules

- number of hits/bats/attempts/bounces
- who has to touch the ball – everyone/one/two/three people

- role of scorer
- different zones for different players

Court/pitch

- size of court
- restricted court size
- open – no limit to playing area

Group

- choice of partner
- choice of group
- number in group

(taken from Wright and Sugden, 1999, p. 22)

The skill of catching can also be broken down into smaller parts – that is, catching can be the subject of *task analysis*. A start can be made by rolling the ball to the child so that they only have to intercept it and not catch it; the parent or teacher could stand very close to them and throw it straight into their arms; or stand further back and bounce the ball so the top of the bounce is at the right place for the child to catch it; a progression can be made to a normal throw and keep varying the distance from the child. Two-handed catching is easier than one hand, stationary catching is easier than moving. By doing this and varying the type of ball used, plus asking for different types of catches, the child is being constantly challenged and yet at the same time they are being helped to progress through the skill-learning process.

This kind of process can be worked out for nearly all activities. For example, when teaching writing, the writing implement can be adapted; lines on the paper inserted, slope of the table modified to make it easier for the child. In addition, the task can be analysed and broken down by concentrating on different processes at different times: posture, angle of the paper, grip of the pencil, formation of letters, size of letters, slope of letters. Sometimes it is only necessary to see the finished product to determine what is necessary (e.g. letters sloping in different directions). At other times it may be necessary to observe the child in the act of writing to determine needs (e.g. noting whether a child starts and finishes letters in the correct place, something which is necessary for fluent cursive writing).

Expert 'scaffolding'

This term is used to describe the process by which a more accomplished person such as a parent gives support to the child to ensure initial success and gradually withdraws it so the child is taking control of their own learning. Thus, support or scaffolding can take many forms – support, where the parent actually guides the child or part of him such as an arm; support by breaking the task down into smaller parts and then building it back up; support by simplifying the whole task and then making it more complex; support by adapting rules and gradually adding complexity. It may be the adult stands with the child to hold them while they are performing activities such as rolling, applying help at the appropriate time. Thus, scaffolding can be the adding of something more detailed or complex or the withdrawing of support such that the child is taking more control and responsibility for their own learning. Scaffolding is a skilful activity, is something that we do better as we practise it and is a fundamental part of teaching motor skills.

Knowing and doing

When a child has a movement difficulty, it can be for a variety of reasons. A child who has been called 'dyspraxic' will very often have a planning difficulty such as an inability to follow a movement sequence, problems in matching or imitating, difficulty in predicting or anticipating. A child's problems here are in 'knowing' what needs to be done rather than the actual execution. Practice on tasks which allow a child to make decisions and plans are recommended. If the child is confused during gross motor activities like running or following and making decisions, then simple games like 'footprints' can help. Different coloured 'footprints' made out of carpet, vinyl, etc. are placed on the floor and the child is asked to move in a sequence like 'blue to red to green to blue'. Start with very simple ones the child can do and build up to more complex ones involving memory and fast decisions. Planning, knowing and decision-making process can also be helped in tasks which demand more fine motor skills such as manipulation. Again, guidance from a therapist can supply you with a range of these tasks for you to use in your own home.

Another child with movement difficulty may have problems on the 'doing' side of the activity. S/he appears to be able to understand what is required, seems to make good plans, makes quick decisions but has difficulty with the actual performance. In these cases, help is needed in the control of the movement, such as an easier ball to grip and catch, bigger targets to throw at, a modified writing implement making it easier to hold, bigger and more appropriately shaped objects to manipulate, and where necessary actual physical guidance through an activity by a helper. A child may have movement difficulties because of problems in 'knowing', in 'doing' or in both.

The guidelines presented are a selection from a host of activities that are available and it is recommended to start by using a few activities and tasks that are comfortable, which are appropriate to the child's needs and which the child seems to enjoy. Success is a great motivator for both parties. As the child improves, there will be an incentive to find new and different activities and also become more confident in working with the child. At the same time, the child will improve which, in turn, will encourage him/her to carry on, enjoy the activities and the benefits which accompany them. These activities are only indicators of what can be done and other sources are presented at the end of the chapter; in addition, professionals and parents are adept at generating their own appropriate activities that tie in with their particular context.

Priorities

It is often the case that movement difficulties are accompanied by other problems, such as lack of attention, distractibility, poor social interaction, language and cognitive skills. It is a major accomplishment to assign priorities to behaviours that are the most important, the most serious or those that lead to other difficulties. Thus, when devising activities, it is important to view them in terms of the overall needs of the child. Assigning priorities is a skilled activity requiring knowledge of the child and of the domain in which the difficulties exist. For this to be done effectively, professionals and parents will need to engage in a strong dialogue involving total cooperation.

Involving the child

The need to set any intervention in the context of daily living should be stressed throughout. This involves discussions with the parents about the needs of the child, the type of intervention in which to engage and how this can be accommodated in the daily life of the family. There is strong evidence to show that if intervention does not take place within the family routines the chances of success are much diminished. In addition, to the parents it is also advisable to involve the child as much as possible. In their COOP method of intervention (Polatajko et al., 2001a, 2001b), the emphasis is on intervention that is 'client centred' with goals chosen by the child working through a cognitive motor approach to teaching skills (Henderson and Sugden, 1992). Although it is accepted that with children in the early years this may prove to be difficult especially in the two- and three-year-old children, it is advisable at all times to take into account the wishes of the child and, if necessary, vary the intervention. By the time a child is five years of age, his/her needs and choices should be given due consideration.

Specific guidelines for working at home and at school

For parents and carers, educational professionals working with children at home and school presents a sense of empowerment, a feeling that they can make a difference and they are not simply dependent upon others. This in turn translates to the child who will take from the situation a positive feeling about themselves. For teachers and other pre school professionals, guidelines can be translated into action within a normal preschool, nursery or classroom environment. Following the summary of guidelines presented above, there is an assumption that parents and educational professionals will have an accurate assessment of the child's strengths and weaknesses and some help from a professional, such as a specialist teacher or therapist. For work at home it is always better to work in conjunction with the school.

In each of the activities described in the following section, examples are presented that illustrate the type of work in which the child could engage. They are not meant to be comprehensive but are typical of developmentally appropriate activities to use. A list of source materials is presented at the end of the chapter; together they provide a comprehensive range of activities for this age range. The activities have been subdivided into groupings that make for ease of organization and include manual skills, handwriting skills, fundamental gross motor skills, self-help skills, ball-game skills and skills in associated behaviours.

Table 5.3 Progression for action

Although each activity that is presented to the child is done with a particular aim in mind, it is recommended that a progression of action is followed, such that a routine for the parent, teacher and child is followed:

- From the assessment process choice of which activities should be prioritized.
- Continuous observation of the child. It is important to note not only whether a child can perform a particular activity but also how it is performed. For this, accurate observation is necessary and, as an aid to this, a recent publication in CD format by the PEA UK called Observing Children Moving (Maude, 2003) is a welcome addition and knowledgeable guide to this process.
- Frequent exposure to the activity. Recall that the first principle of motor learning is that the more appropriate practice the child engages in, the more learning will take place. Thus, as often as possible encourage the child to engage with the task making it part of everyday life.
- More specific teaching if it is deemed necessary presenting different types of movement problem situations.
- Encouraging the child to become an independent learner and problem-solver by the use of varied activities and situations. This will involve the child making decisions and choices.

Table 5.3 provides a progression for any child showing difficulties, allowing a graded response from simple observation and exposure to a choice of activities, through to more detailed and specific teaching encouraging the child to become an independent learner.

The following pages provide examples of activities across a range of movement skills, selecting those that can be adapted for the classroom or for home.

Manual activities

A plan of action can be developed for about a six-week period with actual activities planned every week. This need not be a burdensome task; notes may simply be made of the types of activities that are going to be worked on in the week. It may be that the major activity is manual skills and much of this can be built into the everyday activities that occur in a household. For example, the child may help in the preparation of cooking – very simple tasks like taking food out of packages, laying a table, carrying plates, stacking a dishwasher or wiping clean a surface. Many of these may appear to be household 'chores' but they do prepare a child for life; they are helping the child with general manual skills; they are part of a daily routine occurring in every household and can simply be part of an expectancy of family life. Constant exposure to these is a crucial part of the intervention process.

More formal activities for the improvement of manual skills will involve a brief analysis of the types of manual skills we engage in. For example, a very simple analysis from observation involves the following:

- *One-hand tasks* – where only one hand is involved:
  - object moved within the hand – a coin is moved around the hand using the fingers; a pencil moved in the hand; a door knob is turned using all of the fingers;
  - object is grasped by the hand and fixed – reaching for an object and placing it in another location; use of a writing and drawing implement; pressing a button on a control panel;

- *Two-handed tasks* – where the two hands work together:
  - hands move in a symmetrical manner – they both do the same thing like carrying an object; two-handed catching;
  - hands work asymmetrically – a more usual occurrence, one hand doing one activity to aid the other hand; opening a jar; turning pages of a book; playing a musical instrument; sawing wood; holding a cup while being filled with liquid; various forms of self-help in dressing and washing.

This is a very simple analysis of manual skills and, yet, can lead to quite specific intervention using everyday activities. A point to remember is that children's abilities are often quite specific. For example, a child may be poor at such activities as buttoning and zippers, but may not have a problem with handwriting or vice versa. These are two quite different tasks: handwriting is a continuous visual motor task not involving manipulation of the fingers with one hand holding the page while the other is performing the lead activity. Buttoning, on the other hand, involves both hands and particularly complex finger movements, both dealing with the main object of the task and each one having a complex role.

Thus, from the assessment Checklist, an examination of the manual tasks that need work is required. Below are a number of activities that have proved useful when working with children who have difficulties in manual skills.

Examples of suggested activities can be found in Appendix 2. Other activities include those that are involved in self-help every day. For example, it is always appropriate to include buttons, zips, Velcro fasteners, press studs, lacing, threading and others. Activity boards involving these can be purchased or simply made. In working with these, it is obvious that there are two different activities involved – that of fastening and unfastening, both working with different processes. It is also useful to recognize that activities take on a totally different perspective depending upon the spatial location of the task. For example, fastening a button on a work board which is in front of the child, in full view, is a different activity than buttoning a jacket which is being worn and possibly the button cannot be seen. In the former, the full senses of vision, touch and kinaesthesis are available to the child while in the second only kinaesthesis and touch are available and, as we know from motor learning, in the early part of learning a skill, vision is crucial to the process. Thus, the lesson is that in the first instance the child is taught how to button while vision is available and then when they can do that in a reasonably competent manner move on to a situation where vision is not available. All of these activities can be done at home; they tend to be fun and can be part of everyday life.

Self-help skills

Self-help skills include everyday activities of washing, dressing, toileting and feeding plus activities that involve planning and organizing ranging from packing a lunch box and making sure appropriate books and pencils etc. are ready for school to more complex ones later in childhood such as study skills, organizing time and managing multiple demands. In the early years, there will be a concentration on the washing, feeding, toileting and dressing but it is useful to make preparations for those demands that will appear later.

Handwriting

A very important part of a child's skill repertoire is handwriting and other representational skills. By the age of seven, which is the upper end of our age range, a child should possess handwriting that is legible, if not yet up to full speed and there are a range of progressions a child moves through in order to get to this stage. In Chapter 2, we briefly touched on some of the progressions but a more detailed list is presented below:

Table 5.4 Typical handwriting achievements ages 2 to 7

1. Crude scribbling is usually the beginning of writing and drawing with the child engaging in this at around 2 years of age but there is no apparent plan or coherent design. There is not conclusive evidence to say whether horizontal or vertical scribbles are made first.

2. Spirals start to emerge with repetitive loops and with practice this may produce an overlaid circle with multiple circumferences and a clear centre.

3. During the 3rd and 4th year, the circular movement becomes better controlled and a single imperfect circle starts to be produced.

4. Also at this time, a rudimentary square is attempted, starting with a cross which becomes repetitive and squares emerging in various ways. They can come from spaces left within vertical and horizontal repetitive strokes; they can come from 'squared off' circles or even from following within sides of a paper.

5. By the age of five, children's drawings of circles, squares and rectangles should be clearly separable.

6. A child of five will attempt a triangle but it is not until a child is six that a child can draw a triangle with accuracy and this is followed at seven by a diamond.

Although the table can give a reasonable age and stage progression, it is more important for the order to be correct; for example, it is not useful teaching a triangle if a child cannot draw a square. The order, although not immutable, tends to be circle-square-triangle-diamond.

Many of the shapes described above are used in the printing and writing of letters. By the age of four, children are making attempts to do this and by five, many children can print their first name and by six, can print the alphabet. In the sixth and seventh years the letters are aligned horizontally, as are numbers. As children mature, the size of their writing changes: a five year old is likely to produce letters and numbers about half an inch high and by seven this has reduced to a quarter of an inch.

Many children will have their own way of writing, it can be described as their own style, eventually becoming their trademark. Although reversals of letters and numbers have become a symbol of a problem for a child, it should be remembered that around half of all five year olds will reverse letters and numbers at some time. Thus, if a child of five reverses occasionally this should not necessarily be seen as a problem but if it is continuous and is still present at seven years of age, when only 10 per cent will show reversals, it would be prudent to investigate further.

Examples of suggested handwriting activities can be found in Appendix 2.

As the child progresses, more formal instruction for handwriting should be given. There is evidence to show that handwriting is not taught in a systematic manner in many schools, and despite the advent of computer technology, it is still a fundamental skill needing great attention. It is not the object of this text to cover handwriting in detail, but there are good guidelines from other texts such as Rosemary Sassoon's (2003) 2nd edition excellent text entitled *Handwriting: The Way to Teach It* and the National Handwriting Association (formally the Handwriting Interest Group) which provides a journal and other publications on both research and practice in the handwriting area.

The activities provide the guidelines for any intervention programme; it is probable that many children with movement difficulties have delays as measured against the benchmarks noted above. However, it is the progression that is important; for example, one would not try to teach drawing a triangle before a square or a circle.

The specific case of writing

Rosemary Sassoon (2003) notes that pre-writing exercises are useful but the best way to prepare for handwriting is to teach the simplest letters as early as possible. There is the problem that too early may lead to engrained faults but appropriate instruction, praise and encouragement will help to overcome this. Overall, the advantages of teaching as soon as the child is ready outweigh the disadvantages.

There are a number of different handwriting models and the choice should be a whole school approach to ensure consistency. Sassoon encourages a style with all letters that terminate on the baseline having an exit stroke which promotes flow into the next letter. When cursive writing is introduced, it facilitates a seamless transition between printed and cursive texts. It is not necessary for writing to be continually cursive; very often this makes added unnecessary difficulty for the child. Having logical breaks in words often aids neatness while retaining some emphasis on speed.

With a child showing difficulties, it is useful to watch the child actually writing so that an analysis of the following can be made:

• posture
• appropriate furniture
• position of paper on desk
• pen grip
• choice of pen

When introducing writing in the early years, care and attention should be paid to:

- concept of writing (e.g. left to right; top to bottom)
- spacing
- height differentials
- capitals/small letters
- starting point for each letter
- direction within a letter
- families of letters

Much of the advice here is elaborated in Sassoon's text *Handwriting: The Way to Teach It* (2nd edition) (2003).

Fundamental skills

It has been stressed throughout the book that the early years are the crucial ones for the establishment of the fundamental skills that provide the basis for sport and recreation activities that evolve later. These fundamental skills are part of any movement experience, whether they are performed at home or in the school situation. These activities include:

Running	Walking
Jumping	Hopping
Skipping	Galloping

All should be present in the early years movement experience and each one can be enhanced by:

- frequent exposure in the home or school situation;
- accurate observation by parent or teacher;
- more specific teaching if it is deemed necessary.

If jumping is taken as an example, a progression for a standing broad jump may include the following:

- Decide how long you would wish to work on this skill
- Assess the level of a particular child
  - observe arm action – is it coordinated with legs?
  - any difficulty taking off and landing on both feet?
  - are knees bent on takeoff?
  - is there control on landing?
  - does the trunk lean forward?
- Present numerous situations allowing the child to jump over carpet tiles, over low objects

- Take one or at most two aspects to work on
  - e.g. coordinated use of arms and legs
  - feet staying together throughout the jump
  - bending knees on takeoff
  - stretch and lean forward

Present situations that allow the child to use the jump in different ways.
'Can you jump......'

- *as far as possible?*
- *as quickly as possible?*
- *one after another?*
- *slow then quick jumps?*
- *sideways, backwards?*
- *like a rabbit, frog?*
- *while holding a ball?*

Thus, each activity has a *given sequence of presentation*. The *first is simple exposure* and often that is enough for the child to progress; if there is no progression, work on one or two areas where the child seems to be having difficulty; this is followed by presenting situations in different ways and finally there are challenges to perform the jump in a variety of manners.

Another example could be hopping:

- Decide upon the length of activity time
- Accurately assess through observation:
  - *Is balance held throughout the hop?*
  - *Is action limited to one or two hops?*
  - *Do arms help?*
  - *Is the body upright?*
- Present the action in different situations
  - *Use both legs*
  - *Try for rhythm in hopping*
  - *Do not emphasize speed or distance*
  - *Concentrate on control*
  - *Hop over objects*

Balance and agility activities can be found in Appendix 2.

Fundamental skill activity games

These can be obtained from many sources such as Gallahue and include such games as Red Light, Frozen, Tag, Crows and Cranes, Squirrels in the Trees, Colours, Magic Spots and many others.

Throwing and catching

Ball games are an important part of physical activities at both home and school and are the fundamental skills necessary for participation in many recreational activities. It is also known that these recreational activities encourage other desirable behaviours including social, cognitive and language skills.

Throwing takes many forms, being able to be performed underhand or overhand and in a sidearm pattern but the overarm throw is the one that is most frequently used after the very early stages and the one that is most useful in recreational activities. Again, the sequence of events for any throwing activities is the same as used for the fundamental skills:

- Decide how long the activity will be worked on
- Accurately assess the child through observation
  - *What is the body position-side or front on?*
  - *Is the release appropriate-too early or too late?*
  - *Trunk actions-any rotation?*
  - *Any step forward-appropriate leg?*
- Present numerous situations to encourage throwing
  - *Carpet tiles to encourage step*
  - *Lots of balls, and other throwing objects-bean bags etc*
  - *Throw at targets*
  - *Work for distance and accurately at the same time*
  - *Gradually increase distance and decrease any target size*
  - *Loads of opportunities for practice*

Catching

An obvious activity is to use throwing and catching together; however, it must be remembered that children are not nearly as good as adults at gauging the throwing to the capabilities of the child catching. For this reason, it is crucial to show how to throw for another child to catch and many times the adult will always have to do the throwing until it improves to a standard that can accommodate the catching of a child with difficulties.

- Present many catching opportunities – how long?
- Through observation accurately assess children during catching
  - *Does the child turn away when catching?*
  - *Does the child use the body to catch?*
  - *Are palms held upwards?*
  - *Are arms extended in front of the body?*

- *How are fingers held-tense or relaxed?*
- *How much movement of the body in anticipation*
• Present many opportunities and practices
  - *Move hands to ball*
  - *'Give' in the fingers-use soft objects*
  - *Visually follow the ball*
  - *Move to ball*
  - *Provide verbal clues for the child 'ready-catch'*
  - *Begin with small balls and decrease in size*
  - *Bounce ball on floor to slow it down*
  - *Make sure ball stands out against background*
  - *Vary speed, level and trajectory of the ball*

There are a plethora of activities that can be presented and our experience is that teachers and parents are good at inventing new practices that are peculiar to their situation. Of course, a progression for both throwing and catching is to move them into game situations and these will be useful activities, particularly at the upper age range of the early years group. Simple games such as passing a large ball to each other – a kind of ball skills musical chairs. Other, more complex games, such as those played against a wall – simple throwing and catching to oneself, either with or without bounce. Other games that can be done by a child on their own include simple throwing up in the air and catching with two hands using a large ball progressing through smaller balls to eventually doing this with one hand. Simple bouncing of a large ball with two hands then one hand, then with a smaller ball and eventually moving around while bouncing a ball. As the child progresses from movement for themselves to movement with others, additional qualities are required for this kind of participation, such as an awareness of the other child leading to cooperation.

Activities for ball skills can be found in Appendix 2.

Associated behaviours

There is an abundance of evidence to support the proposition that coordination disorders do not normally occur in isolation, that in many instances they occur in association with other difficulties. These difficulties are often described as being comorbid conditions and, as such, they are seen as part of a general condition involving developmental disabilities such as attention deficit disorder, dyslexia, autistic spectrum disorder and the one that is being discussed here on – Developmental Coordination Disorder. Indeed, such are the overlaps seen that researchers such as Kaplan and colleagues (2001) have described the conditions as being 'atypical brain development' and note that there are few 'pure' single conditions, the vast majority being comorbid conditions of varying degrees. While we believe this label is less than helpful as it is so non specific, it does alert us to the fact that 'pure' coordination disorder is probably the exception rather than the rule.

How does this affect the type of intervention that is presented? Essentially, it points to the overall aim or goal of a particular activity or lesson. What is the outcome of any lesson? In any lesson, one can argue, that there is a continuum of outcomes that range from *learning to move to moving to learn*. It is not simply about education of the physical but also education through the physical of those other naturally developing attributes such as personal and social skills, emotional development, language and cognition.

Any child with coordination difficulties would normally be expected to be engaged in *learning how to move*. This is intrinsically their major problem and, in later years, would be a major component of any physical education programme. All of the activities and programmes that have been presented have been geared to this aim. Thus, in the early years the aim would be to equip the child with all of the major fundamental motor skills that have been chronicled throughout the book. These range from the control of fundamental movements such as posture or locomotion to movement problems that involve planning and strategies in relation to environmental movement problems.

Movement to learn involves learning through movement experiences. A simple example illustrates the essence of this. In a classroom situation, two boys may have movement difficulties but they also have behaviour problems. Thus, it is not simply that the boys have coordination problems but their inappropriate behaviour is adding to their difficulties. An activity that encapsulates this could be a simple task that involve a bench and all the boys have to do is move from opposite ends of the bench, pass in the middle and arrive at the opposite end without either falling off. In order to accomplish this, the boys have to do something in addition to being skilled in movement; they have to cooperate. To cross in the middle, the boys have to hold on to each other in order to cross on the narrow bench without either falling off, and the task is only successfully completed if both boys reach the opposite end. Thus, the boys have to cooperate – an activity that was not one that appeared naturally in their repertoire but one that would be a desirable extra goal.

The bench example is just one of many. Other situations can be created whereby children have to cooperate with each other; where they have to support each other; where without the dual roles the task cannot be accomplished. These examples include activities whereby the child has to use perception and cognition as well as their motor skill in order to accomplish the task. For example, a child may be asked to go through an obstacle course whereby s/he has to move through a blue hoop, crawl under a table or over the square mat. In these instances, the child is being asked to make cognitive and perceptual judgements as well as the motor act to accomplish the task. A further example could be in the area of language. A child may be asked to verbalize what they are doing as well as perform it or another variation may be to watch another child perform and then describe what has happened to another group of children so that they can accomplish the task.

Thus, in any session that involves physical activity there is this continuum from learning to move to moving to learn. It is probable that in any lesson or home situation both of these aims play a prominent role. It is the balance of these two that is important and this balance or ratio will differ according to the needs of the child. In a child whose sole problem is coordination, the learning to move part, while not being the totality of the lesson, will predominate. Similarly, a child who has coordination difficulties but has also been diagnosed as having Asperger's Syndrome where social skills are lacking, the situation becomes different. The activities and situations are designed such that the social skills problem is being addressed as well as the coordination difficulties, with the result that all activities will have a social component where the child has to cooperate in some way with another. All of this is played through a movement situation as it is believed that movement is so motivating that the context encourages appropriate behaviours that may not be easily brought out in other non-movement situations.

Final thoughts: a 'developmental coach'?

One of the constant issues that is raised, particularly by parents, is the confusing array of advice that they receive. Many stories are prevalent about how parents are moved from professional to consultant to expert and back again. It is not simply that this leads to a confusing state of affairs but probably the more important point is that it can lead to parents feeling they have a lack of authority, expertise or even involvement in the whole process. This is not an easy issue to deal with because of the lack of consistency across the country with education and health, both in the public, private and charitable sectors, having views.

Our view is that someone must take responsibility for this state of affairs and become the 'developmental coach'. Just as the coach of a sporting team is responsible for looking at the total input to the team in order to produce the most effective outcome, so the developmental coach engages in the same process for the child with difficulties. There will be multiple inputs and these need to be evaluated with respect to the other relevant factors to produce an outcome that is the line of best fit, according to the lifestyle of the child and immediate significant family and friends.

Our view is that intervention should be a normal part of daily life. It should blend naturally into the home situation, not being a specific chore that has to be done. At school, it is done as part of the daily routine of a normal classroom. *It is our firm belief that if intervention is not part of the child and family daily life, the chances of success are minimal.*

For these reasons it is firmly believed that the *parents and caregivers* are the most appropriate individuals to be the *developmental coach*. This is not without difficulties; the most obvious being that parents do not usually have the expertise to evaluate all of the possibilities. However, as noted at the beginning of the chapter, parents have the two major advantages of knowing the child better than anyone else and seeing them on a daily basis. In addition, parents have a huge vested interest and know the circumstances better than anyone else in which the child has to function. The issue then becomes how professionals can deliver advice, guidance and practical help, such that parents can take up this role and carry out effectively. It is incumbent upon professionals in the health and educational fields to modify their practice such that they cascade some of their skills to parents, enabling parents to make the most appropriate decisions with respect to their child functioning in the context of daily family life.

Addresses and other sources of help

Hunt P (ed) (1998) Praxis Makes Perfect II. Hitchin, Herts: Dyspraxia Foundation.

Kirby A (1999) Dyspraxia The Hidden Handicap. London: Souvenir Press.

Kirby A, Drew S (2002) Guide to Dyspraxia and Developmental Coordination Disorders. London: David Fulton Publishers.

Macintyre C (2000) Dyspraxia in the Early Years. London: David Fulton Publishers.

Macintyre C (2001) Dyspraxia 5–11. London: David Fulton Publishers.

National Handwriting Association (NIHA) Contact: Rita Mechen, NRA Administrator, 12 Isis Avenue, Bicester, Oxon. OX26 2GS. Email: admin.nha@ntlworld.com; Website: http://www.nha-handwriting.org.uk.

Portwood M (1999) (2nd Edition) Developmental Dyspraxia. London: David Fulton Publishers.

Ripley K, Dames B, Barrett J (1999) Dyspraxia: A Guide for Teachers and Parents. London: David Fulton Publishers.

Sugden DA, Wright HC (1998) Motor Coordination Disorders in Children. Thousand Oaks, CA.: Sage.

Sugden DA, Wright HC, Chambers ME, Markee A (2002) Developmental Coordination Disorder: A booklet for parents and teachers. Leeds: University of Leeds.

Technical information

An investigation using the Early Years Movement Skills Checklist to identify children with movement skill difficulties

Thirty-four schools in three Local Education Authorities were randomly selected to participate in the study. This random sample consisted of 24 nursery schools/classes, 25 reception classes, and 22 Year 1 classes and involved 71 class teachers. Checklists taken to schools included 144 for 3 year olds, 150 for 4 year olds, and 132 for 5 and 6 year olds. Overall, 426 Early Years Movement Skills Checklists were distributed in 34 schools.

Procedure

The Early Years Movement Skills Checklists were taken to the schools, along with an explanation of the aims and purpose of the Checklist, and instructions for administering and scoring the Checklist. Each teacher was asked to choose three girls and three boys from their class, according to random numbers supplied with the instructions. In classes where there was more than one adult (for example teaching assistant, nursery nurse, regular parent helper) one extra Checklist was left with the teacher to be completed by the other adult, independently of the teacher, in order to obtain a measure of interrater reliability. A total of 68 Early Years Movement Skills Checklists were left in schools to be completed for this purpose. All the teachers were shown how to use the Early Years Movement Skills Checklist, which were left with them for a period of three weeks. At the end of the three-week period, completed Checklists were collected from each of the schools.

When returning to schools to collect the completed Early Years Movement Skills Checklists, one further Checklist was left with each class teacher, with the request that it was completed on one of the same children one month after the initial Checklist, as a measure of test–retest reliability. A total of 70 Early Years Movement Skills Checklists were left in schools to be completed for this purpose.

In order to obtain a measure of the predictive validity of the Early Years Movement Skills Checklist, a sample from the 4, 5 and 6 year olds was selected for testing on an established test of motor skills. A measure of predictive validity was obtained as it was necessary to find out whether the same children identified by the Early Years Movement Skills Checklist as having movement difficulties, would be identified by an established movement skills test. The selected sample included children whose scores were in the lowest 5 per cent of the total scores of the Checklist (Sample 1), those children whose scores were in the lowest 5–10 per cent of the total scores of the Checklist (Sample 2) and a random sample of 5 per cent of children whose scores were not in the bottom 10 per cent of the total scores of the Checklist (Sample 3). The assessment instrument that was used to measure predictive validity was the test component of the Movement ABC (Henderson and Sugden, 1992).

Results and analysis

Checklists in the main sample

Of the 426 Early Years Movement Skills Checklists taken to schools 422 were returned (99 per cent); two of which were completed for children under three years of age giving 420 (98.5 per cent) as a total number of usable Checklists.

The overall results for the main sample of the Early Years Movement Skills Checklist are shown in Table A1.1. The mean score per item is also

Table A1.1 Mean scores per section, standard deviations and medians

| | 3 year olds | | 4 year olds | | 5 year olds | |
	Boys	Girls	Boys	Girls	Boys	Girls
Section 1	12.29	9.98	8.68	7.74	7.40	6.79
per item	2.05	1.66	1.44	1.29	1.23	1.13
SD	4.36	3.17	2.80	2.58	2.13	1.76
Median	12.00	10.00	8.00	6.00	6.00	6.00
Section 2	8.54	6.65	6.45	6.27	6.18	5.61
per item	1.71	1.33	1.29	1.25	1.24	1.12
SD	3.13	1.90	1.79	2.07	2.04	1.46
Median	8.00	6.00	6.00	5.00	5.00	5.00
Section 3	6.78	5.67	5.90	5.51	5.79	5.42
per item	1.36	1.13	1.18	1.10	1.16	1.08
SD	2.45	1.19	1.67	1.34	1.78	1.46
Median	6.00	5.00	5.00	5.00	5.00	5.00

indicated, being a more accurate reflection of performance, as the number of items that each section contains affects the mean score per section. In addition, the standard deviation and median along with mean scores for each section are presented.

A 2 (gender) by 3 (age) by 4 (section) ANOVA with repeated measures on the last factor was performed on the data. There were main effects for section, $F (3, 1011) = 364$, $p < 0.0001$, gender, $F (1, 64) = 17.325$, $p < 0.0001$; and age, $F (2, 149) = 39.98$, $p < 0.0001$. There was an interaction effect involving section and gender, $F (3, 15.62) = 5.64$, $p < 0.0001$ (Figure A1.1) and an interaction effect involving section and age, $F (6, 71.96) = 38.94$, $p < 0.0001$ (Figure A1.2). All interactions were further analysed using simple main effects and Tukey's HSD Test. There was a significant difference between gender in Sections 1, 2 and 3 but not in 4 and, where there was a difference, the boys scored higher (poorer) than the

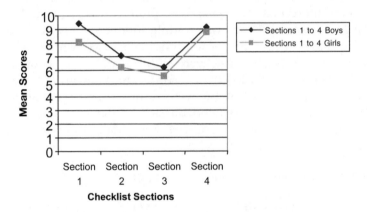

Figure A1.1 Interaction of section and gender.

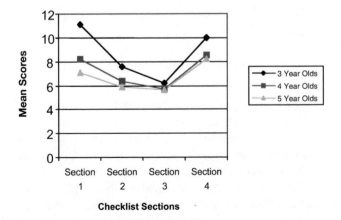

Figure A1.2 Interaction of section and age.

girls. There was an interaction between age and section showing significant differences between the 3-year-old children and the 4- and 5-year-old
children for Sections 1, 2 and 4. The 3-year-old children scored poorer
than the 4-year-old children who, in turn, scored poorer than the 5-year-
old children. These interaction effects are shown in Figures A1.1 and A1.2.

Reliability of the Early Years Movement Skills Checklist

The reliability of the Checklist was examined in two ways – interrater reliability and test–retest reliability.

Interrater reliability

When the Early Years Movement Skills Checklists were taken to schools to
be completed for the main sample, one additional Checklist was left in
classes where there was more than one adult. It was requested that this
Checklist be completed by the other adult, independently of the teacher,
in order to obtain a measure of interrater reliability. A total of 68 Early
Years Movement Skills Checklists were left in schools to be completed for
use as an interrater reliability measure. Thirty-seven (54 per cent)
Checklists for interrater reliability were returned and correlations were
performed on the scores obtained in each of the four sections of the
Checklist and on the total of Sections 1 to 4. Pearson's product-moment
correlations are shown in Table A1.2.

Table A1.2 Interrater reliability coefficients of the Checklist

| | 3 year olds | | 4 year olds | | 5 year olds | |
	Boys	Girls	Boys	Girls	Boys	Girls
Section 1	0.97	0.94	0.46	0.94	0.81	1.00
Section 2	0.93	0.95	1.00	1.00	0.93	0.88
Section 3	0.95	0.58	1.00	0.99	0.80	1.00
Section 4	0.91	0.76	0.58	0.98	0.80	0.82
1–4 Total	0.98	0.80	0.84	0.98	0.95	0.95

All the correlations are significant at the 0.01 level except for the score
for four-year-old boys on Section 1, which is significant at the 0.05 level.
The number of interrater reliability Checklists returned for four-year-old
boys was small (4) and, even though agreement between the two sets of
data was good, a difference of 4 points for 1 child for the total of Section
1 made a large difference to the statistical analysis. In addition to the
above correlation coefficients, the correlation for the group as a whole
was computed. The total score yielded a correlation coefficient of 0.96,

which is highly significant ($p < 0.01$). The same correlation coefficients were computed for individual sections; the correlation coefficients were 0.94 for Section 1, 0.93 for Section 2, 0.91 for Section 3 and 0.87 for Section 4. All of these correlations are statistically significant ($p < 0.01$). Overall, the results of the interrater reliability are very encouraging with 61 per cent of the scores over 0.90, 83 per cent of the scores over 0.80, and only one, 0.46 for Section 1 for the four-year-old boys, being low.

Test–retest reliability

When returning to schools to collect the completed Early Years Movement Skills Checklists, one further Checklist was left with each class teacher, with the request that it was completed on one of the same children one month after the initial Checklist, as a measure of test–retest reliability. A total of 70 Early Years Movement Skills Checklists were left in schools to be completed for this purpose, and 68 (97 per cent) were returned. Correlations were performed on each of the four sections of the Checklist and on the total of Sections 1 to 4. Pearson's product-moment correlations are shown in Table A1.3.

Table A1.3 Test-retest reliability coefficients of the Checklist

| | 3 year olds | | 4 year olds | | 5 year olds | |
	Boys	Girls	Boys	Girls	Boys	Girls
Section 1	0.93	0.76	0.94	0.98	0.92	0.87
Section 2	0.87	0.92	0.83	1.00	0.89	0.34
Section 3	0.90	0.96	0.68	1.00	0.64	0.96
Section 4	0.97	0.87	0.82	0.99	0.75	0.95
1–4 Total	0.96	0.90	0.90	1.00	0.89	0.98

All the correlations are significant at the 0.01 level, except for the five-year-old girls on Section 2, which is significant at the 0.05 level. There was strong agreement between the two sets of Checklists for the five-year-old girls; however, the two sets of scores showed a difference of a few points and with such a small number of subjects (4) these few points make a large difference to the statistical analysis. In addition, this group had low scores with smaller ranges than other groups, which would tend to depress the correlation coefficient even though there was strong agreement between the two sets of data. Overall, the results of the test–retest reliability are very encouraging with 60 per cent of the scores over 0.90, 84 per cent of the scores over 0.80, and only one, 0.34 for Section 2 for the five-year-old girls, being low. In addition to the above correlation coefficients, the correlation coefficient for the group as a whole was computed. The total score yielded a correlation coefficient of 0.95, which is highly significant ($p < 0.01$). The same correlation coefficients were computed for individual sections; the correlation coefficients were 0.92 for Section 1, 0.88 for Section 2, 0.84 for Section 3 and 0.93 for Section 4. All of these correlations are statistically significant ($p < 0.01$).

Stability of Checklists in the reliability study

The stability of total scores on the Checklists used in the reliability study was another measure of reliability which was calculated. This involved examining the interrater Checklists and the test–retest Checklists and comparing the total scores for each pair of Checklists. The original Checklists were assigned to three categories: those whose total scores on the Checklist were in the lowest 5 per cent, those whose total scores were in the lowest 5–10 per cent and those whose total scores were not in the lowest 10 per cent.

The Checklists used in the reliability study were examined to determine to what extent, if any, each pair changed category. Of the 37 Checklists used for the interrater reliability measure, three interrater Checklists placed children in a different category from the original Checklist: two Checklists originally had total scores of 39 and 41 which placed them in the lowest 5–10 per cent, while the interrater Checklists both had total scores of 42, which changed the category to the lowest 5 per cent. One Checklist originally had a total score of 37 which placed it in the lowest 5–10 per cent, while the interrater Checklist had a total of 34, which changed the category to those outside of the lowest 10 per cent of scores. All other interrater Checklists remained in the original categories. The results indicated 91.8 per cent agreement for the interrater reliability Checklists.

Of the test–retest Checklists, 5 out of 68 placed children in a different category from the original category. Two Checklists originally had total scores of 32 and 36, which placed them in the category outside of the lowest 10 per cent, while the test–retest Checklists had total scores of 37 and 41 respectively, placing them in the lowest 5–10 per cent category. Two Checklists originally had total scores in the lowest 5 per cent (44 and 42), while the test–retest Checklists placed both in the category outside of the lowest 10 per cent, scoring 35 and 33 respectively. One Checklist which had originally been placed in the lowest 5–10 per cent, was placed by the test–retest Checklist in the lowest 5 per cent; the total score having changed from 39 to 42. All other test–retest Checklists remained in the original categories. The results indicated a 92.6 per cent agreement for the test–retest reliability Checklists. This measure of reliability is, once again, encouraging.

While it is acknowledged that the reliability studies involved small samples, a tentative conclusion is that the overall reliability of the Early Years Movement Skills Checklist could be considered to be good.

Validity of the Early Years Movement Skills Checklist

In this study, the focus of the measure of the predictive validity is whether children identified in the lowest 5 per cent on the Checklist will also obtain a score in the same range on another assessment instrument, and similarly for children in the lowest 5–10 per cent and children in the random 5 per cent. The assessment instrument which was used to compare consistency was the Movement ABC (Henderson and Sugden, 1992).

Selection of children for the validity study

A sample from the 4, 5 and 6 year olds was selected for testing on the Movement ABC (Henderson and Sugden, 1992). The selected sample included children whose total scores on the Checklist were in the lowest 5 per cent (Sample 1), those children whose total scores were in the lowest 5–10 per cent (Sample 2) and a random sample of 5 per cent of children whose total scores were not in the bottom 10 per cent (Sample 3). 298 Checklists were returned for the 4, 5 and 6 year old children, therefore, each of the 3 sample groups would consist of 15 children; giving a total of 45 children to be tested.

The selected sample

The scores for Sample 1 (lowest 5 per cent) ranged from 60 to 42, and, as there were 5 children with scores of 42, the total number of children with the lowest scores was 17. The scores for Sample 2 (lowest 5–10 per cent) ranged from 41 to 37, and, again, 6 children had scores of 37, bringing the total in this group to 16. For Sample 3 (randomly selected group), a random set of numbers was generated by a computer programe which identified 16 children whose scores were not in the lowest 10 per cent. The scores of this group were at or below 32. The total number of children identified for testing on the Movement ABC (Henderson and Sugden, 1992) was 49. However, due to drop out, children leaving the area and non-cooperation this number was reduced to 45 (15 in Sample 1, 14 in Sample 2 and 16 in Sample 3). The mean age of Sample 1 was 62.33 months (SD 6.72 months), Sample 2 was 61.07 months (SD 7.99 months) and Sample 3 was 65.06 months (SD 6.79 months).

A 3 (group) by 4 (section) ANOVA with repeated measures on the last factor was performed on the selected sample. The analysis provided a main effect for section, F $(3,150)$ = 30.37 ($p < 0.0001$ and for group, F $(2, 120)$ = 122.20 $p < 0.0001$ with the children in Sample 1 (lowest 5 per cent) scoring higher (poorer). There was also an interaction involving section and group, F $(3, 25.71)$ = 5.37 $p < 0.0001$ and the nature of this interaction was examined using simple main effects and Tukey's HSD test. In all of the sections there were significant differences between the three groups, where the children in Sample 1 scored poorer than the children in Sample 2 who in turn, scored poorer than the children in Sample 3. These results are shown in Figure A1.3.

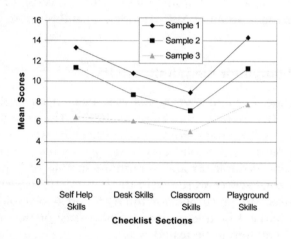

Figure A1.3 Interaction of section and the selected sample.

Comparison with the Movement ABC

All of the children in the three groups were tested with the Movement ABC Test (Henderson and Sugden, 1992) and the results are reported and analysed below. Table A1.4 shows the comparative results of the mean test total and section scores, along with the standard deviation and median for each section in the Movement ABC. As with the Checklist scores, the mean score per item is also indicated, as this is a more accurate reflection of performance, as the number of items that each section contains affects the mean score per section.

A 3 (group) by 3 (section) ANOVA with repeated measures on the last factor was performed on the data for the Movement ABC Test scores. As expected, the analysis provided a main effect for section, F $(2, 75.66)$ = 17.71 $p < 0.0001$ and for group, F $(2, 112.41)$ = 29.22 $p < 0.0001$. There was an interaction effect involving group and section, F $(4, 36.42)$ = 8.52

Table A1.4 Mean section and item scores, total scores, SD and medians on the Movement ABC Test

	Sample 1	Sample 2	Sample 3
Manual dexterity			
Mean	6.77	1.61	1.47
Per item	2.57	0.54	0.49
SD	4.87	2.13	1.54
Median	7.00	1.25	1.00
Ball skills			
Mean	3.60	2.86	0.25
Per item	1.80	1.43	0.12
SD	1.84	2.21	0.58
Median	3.00	2.00	0.00
Balance			
Mean	8.23	5.50	0.72
Per item	2.74	1.83	1.24
SD	2.88	3.37	1.57
Median	8.50	6.75	0.00
Total score			
Mean	18.60	9.96	2.44
SD	6.92	5.35	2.69
Median	18.50	11.25	1.50

$p < 0.0001$ with significant differences between the three groups for Static and Dynamic Balance. Tukey's HSD Test also revealed significant differences between Sample 1 and Sample 2 for Manual Dexterity and there were also significant differences between Sample 1 and Sample 3 and Sample 2 and Sample 3 for Ball Skills. In each case, Sample 1 scored poorer than Sample 2 who scored poorer than Sample 3.

Stability of the groupings

While the groupings as a whole confirm the groupings identified by the Checklist, it is necessary to look at individual Movement ABC Test profiles. The Movement ABC Test scores are interpreted in the light of percentile norms; scores below the 5th percentile should be considered as indicative of a movement problem while scores between the 5th and 15th percentile suggest a degree of difficulty that is borderline. For the purpose of this study scores between the 5th and 10th percentile have been considered, as the children in the validity study scored in the lowest 5 per cent of the Checklist and the lowest 5–10 per cent of the Checklist. The percentile norms are divided into two age groups (4–5 years of age and 6 years and above): the 5th percentile cut-off point for age 4 and 5 years is 17 and 13.5 for 6 years and above. At the 10th percentile, the cut-off points for age 4 and 5 years is 13 and 11.5/11 for 6 years and above.

Movement ABC Test scores of the children in Sample 1 placed 9 out of 15 children (60 per cent) at or below the 5th percentile, 4 out of 15 (27 per cent) between the 5th and 10th percentile and 2 out of 15 (13 per cent) above the 10th percentile. Test scores of the children in Sample 2 placed 3 out of 14 (21 per cent) at or below the 5th percentile, 4 out of 14 (29 per cent) between the 5th and 10th percentile and 7 out of 14 (50 per cent) above the 10th percentile. Test scores of the children in Sample 3 placed all 16 above the 10th percentile.

Correlation of the Checklist with the Movement ABC

Total scores of the Checklist were correlated with total scores on the Movement ABC Test and the Pearson product-moment correlations for each group were as follows: Sample 1: 0.23, Sample 2: 0.57, Sample 3: 0.35 and all the selected sample 0.76. The correlation coefficients for Sample 2 and the whole of the selected sample are significant at the 0.01 level, and the correlation coefficients for Sample 1 and Sample 3 are significant at the 0.05 level. The correlation coefficients for the individual groups are not impressive and not totally unexpected, given the movement of children between groups. The correlation for the whole of the selected sample is encouraging. In summary, it appears that with the more severe problems there is fairly good agreement between the Checklist and the Movement ABC Test; the Checklist identified some children who were not confirmed by the Movement ABC Test, but no children were picked up by the Movement ABC Test who had not previously been identified by the Checklist.

Sensitivity and specificity

Of the 45 children involved in the validity study, 20 of the original 29 were identified by the Movement ABC Test (Henderson and Sugden, 1992) as displaying movement difficulties. Based on this sample of 45 children, the sensitivity index of the Early Years Movement Skills Checklist has been calculated as 1.00. Sixteen children were originally identified as not having movement difficulties, but the Movement ABC Test identified 25 as not having difficulties. Thus, the specificity index has been calculated as 0.64. In practical terms, this means that if a Checklist is positive then 64 times in every 100 the child will have movement difficulties and if a Checklist is negative then the child will not be found to have movement difficulties, meaning that the Checklist is totally accurate in screening out children without difficulties.

Summary and discussions

This study has focused on the identification and assessment of movement difficulties in children aged 3–5 years and specifically on the construction of an assessment instrument which has been designed to be used flexibly by teachers and parents to describe more accurately the problems some children are experiencing in the motor domain.

Validity of the Checklist

Construct and content validity

The Early Years Movement Skills Checklist was constructed to assess functional, everyday skills of 3- to 5-year-old children and, as such, contains activities which are easily observed by teachers and parents as part of everyday activities. Drawing upon the available literature and from professionals in the field a Checklist was developed which contained activities which are functional, everyday skills. This addressed the issue of content validity which concerns the extent to which a measurement is judged to reflect the meaningful elements of a construct or a domain of content and not any extraneous elements (Burton and Miller, 1998). By consulting professionals working in the field, academics, health service professionals and teachers, at every stage of the construction, an attempt was made to ensure that the activities contained in the Checklist are skills which are frequently taught or seen in the early years environment.

Predictive validity

When children in the selected sample were tested on the Movement ABC Test (Henderson and Sugden, 1992) overall mean scores reflected the groupings from the Checklist. However, when individual children's scores were examined in more detail and interpreted in the light of percentile norms, a different picture emerged. Four children from Sample 1 moved to the 5th–10th percentile, and two children moved to above the 10th percentile; three children from Sample 2 moved to the 5th percentile and seven children moved to above the 10th percentile; all the children from Sample 3 remained above the 10th percentile.

An examination of the Movement ABC Test (Henderson and Sugden, 1992) scores for the children who moved categories based on their Test score indicate that they have specific difficulties in one or two areas only, which are not indicated in the overall Test score. For example, one child scored 9.5 on the Test and a closer look at this score reveals that she scored 7.5 for Static and Dynamic Balance tasks. Referring back to the Checklist scores for this child indicates that she had particular difficulties on General Classroom Skills and Recreational/Playground skills – confirming her Test score. Although movement between the categories appears to be quite dramatic, exploration of individual cases reveals that these children are not free of difficulties, but rather, their difficulties are confined to one or two areas only. It may be a case for suggesting that a two-step procedure to identify children with DCD, such as that suggested by Wright and Sugden (1996a), may be required for this age group.

Pearson's product-moment correlations were calculated for the Checklist total scores and the Movement ABC Test scores (Henderson and Sugden, 1992). The correlation for the whole of the selected sample was 0.76 and it appears that with the more severe movement problems there is good agreement between the Checklist and the Test. However, the Checklist identified some children who were not confirmed by the Movement ABC Test (Henderson and Sugden, 1992), but no children were identified by the Test that had not previously been identified by the Checklist.

Reliability of the Checklist

Interrater reliability

Overall, the results of the interrater reliability are very encouraging with 61 per cent of the scores over 0.90 and 83 per cent of the scores over 0.80. It was felt that because of the nature of the scoring of the Checklist, a more accurate measure of reliability would be to measure the correlation coefficient for individual items in each section. Pearson's product-moment correlations were calculated for individual items in each of the five sections. Again, the results of this are very encouraging. The stability of total scores on the Checklists was also evaluated and the results indicated 91.8 per cent agreement for the stability of the Checklists. However, care must be taken when interpreting these results; the Checklists were left in schools with the instruction that the interrater Checklist was completed by another adult independently of the class teacher. It was taken on trust that the interrater Checklist was completed independently, but there is a possibility that some collusion took place between the raters.

Test–retest reliability

The overall results of the test–retest reliability also are very encouraging with 60 per cent of the scores over 0.90 and 84 per cent of the scores over 0.80. As above for the interrater reliability measure, Pearson's product-moment correlations were calculated for individual items on the Checklist. Again, the results are encouraging with 30 per cent of scores over 0.80, and 74 per cent of the scores over 0.70. The stability of the Checklists was also explored and results indicated a 92.6 per cent agreement for the test–retest reliability Checklists. The test–retest measure was completed one month after the original Checklist and with the possibility of class teachers remembering how they have scored the original Checklist, these results are treated with caution.

Performance differences

Differences in performance between ages

The Early Years movement Skills Checklist was constructed for use with children of 3, 4 and 5 years of age and therefore contains activities which it is believed are functional in nature and relevant to children of this age. Developmental differences were found between the three age groups of children on each section of the Checklist – the 3-year-old children had higher scores than the 4-year-old children, who in turn had higher scores than the 5-year-old children. Statistical analysis confirmed these differences between the three age groups: a main effect for age was found with the younger children scoring higher (poorer).

The biggest difference in section scores between the three age groups was seen in Section 1 (Self-Help Skills) with significant differences between the three age groups for this section. Section 1 of the Early Years Movement Skills Checklist assesses self-help skills, and it is well documented that self-help skills such as dressing, grooming and feeding, skills which are contained in the Checklist, require many types of movements (Keogh and Sugden, 1985).

The differences in scores for Section 2 (Desk Skills), Section 3 (General Classroom Skills) and Section 4 (Recreational/Playground Skills) all displayed a similar trend; with a significant difference between the 3-year-old children and the 4- and 5-year-old children but no significant difference between the 4-year-old children and the 5-year-old children.

These differences between the three age groups of children are not unexpected, as from the ages of 2 to 7 children are constantly modifying and elaborating earlier achievements. Within this period of development, the child becomes more consistent, more accurate and better coordinated, with fewer extraneous movements. Force becomes more modulated, and spatial accuracy is fairly good when moving in a stable environment (Keogh and Sugden, 1985).

In view of this, one would expect 5-year-old children to be better able to perform the activities contained in the Checklist and, therefore, have better overall scores than 3-year-old and 4-year-old children. As seen above, this developmental progression is reflected in the total scores for all sections of the Checklist where the 5-year-old children scored consistently better than the 4-year-old children who, in turn, scored consistently better than the 3-year-old children. However, there was no significant difference between the scores of the 4 and 5-year-old children on any individual section apart from Section 1.

Differences in performance between gender

The results for the main sample of the Early Years Movement Skills Checklist have been analysed according to age, gender and section. Mean scores per section and per item were calculated and differences between age and gender were found in all sections of the Checklist. The 3-year-old boys and girls showed the biggest differences in scores for each section of the Checklist and the girls scored consistently lower (better) than the boys, indicating that they were better able to perform tasks. A similar picture has emerged for the other age groups, where the biggest differences in scores between the boys and girls for both the 4-year-olds and the 5-year-olds was found for Section 1. In each of the age groups, the boys had more difficulties than the girls for Section 1, though statistical analysis showed there was a significant difference between the 3-year-old boys and 3-year-old girls, but not between any of the other groups.

In Section 2 (Desk Skills), again the 3-year-old boys displayed the most difficulties and statistical analysis confirmed that there was a significant difference between the 3-year-old boys and the 3-year-old girls for this section, but no significant differences between any of the other groups.

In Section 3 (General Classroom Skills), the picture is similar to that in Sections 1 and 2; the girls in each of the age groups had lower mean scores than the boys. However, statistical analysis revealed that there was no significant difference between any of the groups for Section 3.

A slightly different picture emerges for Section 4 (Recreation and Playground Skills). As in the other three sections, the 3-year-old boys had a higher mean score than the 3-year-old girls and the 5-year-old boys had a higher mean score than the 5-year-old girls, but the 4-year-old boys scored better than the 4-year-old girls. Even though the 3-year-old boys and the 5-year-old boys had higher scores than the girls in these age groups, the differences in their performance scores are small and are not statistically significant.

Section 4 for the 4-year-old children is the only section on the Checklist where the boys had a lower score than the girls. This may be due in part to the nature of Section 4, involving a number of ball skills – a task which boys traditionally perform as well as or better than girls. However, this does not explain why the 3-year-old boys and 5-year-old boys did not score similarly for this section. One observation that has been noted for the 4-year-old children is that, with the exception of the mean score for Section 1, there was very little difference between the mean scores for each section for boys and girls. The total mean scores for Sections 1 to 4 also show the same trend for this group.

Gender differences in early movement development have been checked for many activities and for many children. Before puberty boys show a slight difference for maximum performance tasks (standing broad jump) whereas girls show a similar advantage in control areas.

Differences in performance of the selected sample

The selected sample consisted of those children whose scores fell within the lowest 5 per cent, the lowest 5–10 per cent and a random 5 per cent of children whose scores were not in the lowest 10 per cent. The Checklist scores obtained for children in the selected sample followed the expected pattern – the children in Sample 1 scored higher (poorer) than the children in Sample 2 who scored higher than the children in Sample 3.

This analysis of performance differences between the three age groups shows developmental differences with the 3-year-old children scoring higher (poorer) than the 4-year-old children, who, in turn, scored higher (poorer) than the 5-year-old children. However, the minimum score for each of the three age groups on the Checklist was found to be 23. Essentially, this indicates that there are 3- and 4-year-old children who are able to perform the activities as well as the 5-year-old children. Two explanations could account for this. First, there could be a ceiling on the Checklist with no way for older, more competent children to improve and second, some children attended private day care nursery from 6 months of age and have considerable experience of these types of activities.

Conclusions

The Early Years Movement Skills Checklist was constructed using functional, everyday skills appropriate for 3- to 5-year-old children and is organized into four sections, each one focusing on a specific area of functional, everyday activities. In this way, it is possible to identify specific environments in which a child experiences difficulties and enables a child's difficulties to be assessed appropriately. For some children, their difficulties encompass all areas of functioning, while for others their difficulties may be apparent in one or two areas only and the Checklist is able to distinguish between these children and can specify the nature of the difficulties experienced by each individual child.

The Early Years Movement Skills Checklist is able to differentiate between children with movement difficulties and those without movement difficulties. The children identified as displaying movement difficulties were found to be a significantly different group from their well coordinated peers. In addition, it shows developmental progression of children aged 3–5 years.

Combining the two sources of information, the Early Years Movement Skills Checklist and the Movement ABC Test (Henderson and Sugden, 1992), the information which is gained gives a reasonably complete picture of the difficulties individual children experience. Using the information in this way, it was noted that 4 per cent of children were found to have serious difficulties with movement skills and a further 3 per cent were found to be 'at risk'.

Overall, it is concluded that the Early Years Movement Skills Checklist can be used as a screening procedure. As noted above, all of the children identified by the Checklist as not having movement difficulties were confirmed by the Movement ABC Test (Henderson and Sugden, 1992) as not displaying difficulties. However, a small number of children identified by the Early Years Movement Skills Checklist as displaying movement difficulties were not confirmed by this standardized procedure as displaying movement difficulties. It is suggested that the Early Years Movement Skills Checklist can be used carefully by teachers, parents, physiotherapists and occupational therapists as an aid to diagnoses and management of movement difficulties in young children.

Early years movement skills checklist

The Early Years Movement Skills checklist and related materials are available free to purchasers of the print version. Visit the website http://www.wiley.com/go/checklist to find out how to access and download these resources.

Administration and interpretation of the checklist

The Early Years Movement Skills Checklist (see overleaf) is an instrument which has been designed to be used flexibly by teachers, parents and other professionals involved with children showing movement difficulties. The aim has been to design an efficient, speedy and accurate instrument to aid in the identification and assessment of young children (3–5 years of age) with movement difficulties. It is a functional checklist which has been designed to be completed as part of the teacher's daily routine, obtaining a measure of the child's typical patterns of functioning in familiar and representative environments, such as home and school.

There are four parts to the Checklist. The focus of assessment in each section is as follows:

Section 1   Self help skills
Section 2   Desk skills
Section 3   General classroom skills
Section 4   Recreational/Playground skills

Administering and scoring the checklist

The focus of interest is how a child performs a task on a daily basis and therefore the Checklist contains items which can be observed by teachers and/or parents as part of the child's daily routine. It has been designed to be completed from memory or filled in over a period of one to two weeks to allow for careful observation of the child in the classroom and the playground.

EARLY YEARS MOVEMENT SKILLS CHECKLIST

Name .... Gender .... Date of birth ....
School .... Age ....y .... m
Assessed by .... Date of Test .... Class ....

Section 1	Section 2	Section 3	Section 4	Total	

Can Do		Cannot Do	
Well	Just	Almost	Not Close
1	2	3	4

SECTION 1 Self Help Skills

The child can

- Put on a T-shirt without assistance ....
- Take off a T-shirt without assistance ....
- Fasten accessible coat buttons ....
- Unfasten accessible coat buttons ....
- Feed self using fork and spoon ....
- Wash and dry hands ....

Section 1 Total ....

SECTION 2 Desk Skills

The child can

- Copy a circle and a cross from a completed example ....
- Pick up and place pieces in an interlocking jigsaw ....
- Turn single pages of a book ....
- Use scissors to cut across a piece of paper (e.g. 4" strip) ....
- Construct simple models using duplo, lego, megablocks ....

Section 2 Total ....

Can Do		Cannot Do	
Well	Just	Almost	Not Close
1	2	3	4

SECTION 3 General Classroom Skills

The child can

- Sit on the floor with legs crossed and back straight ....
- Carry books and toys across the classroom in order to put away ....
- Move around the classroom/school avoiding collision with stationary people/objects ....
- Move around the classroom/school avoiding collision with moving people/objects ....
- Move forward, backward, sideways, under and over when shown ....

                                    Section 3 Total   ....

SECTION 4 Recreational/Playground Skills

The child can

- Use fixed playground equipment (e.g. climbing frame, slide) ....
- Ride a variety of moving vehicles (e.g. pedal car, tricycle) ....
- Kick a large stationary ball ....
- Throw a large ball overarm using both hands ....
- Join in playground activities, demonstrating running and jumping ....
- Walk on tip toes for 4 steps ....
- Catch a large (10") ball with two hands ....

                                    Section 4 Total   ....

Sections 1–4

The Checklist is a criterion referenced assessment instrument and for each of the tasks included in Sections 1 to 4 there are four alternative responses which describe how well the child deals with the task:

Can Do		Cannot Do	
Well	Just	Almost	Not Close
1	2	3	4

First, it is necessary to decide whether the child *can* or *cannot* do the task. Then, consider how well they perform. If the child *can* do it, can they perform it 'Well' or only 'Just'? If the child *cannot* perform the task, can they 'Almost' do it or are they 'Not Close'?

Please rate the child on how s/he performs the task not on whether s/he is good or not so good for his/her age. Each item requires a single overall rating. The responses to each of the activities are scored on a four-point scale from 1 ('Well') to 4 ('Not Close'). Select the response for each activity that best describes the child being assessed and enter the score on the Checklist. Scores for each section are then added and the result entered at the end of the section. These four separate totals are then entered in the summary box at the beginning of the Checklist and summed to achieve an overall score.

Checklist interpretation

If a child scores in the lowest 5 per cent for their age group, it is recommended that action is taken to help the child. Details concerning this are given in Chapter 5. Between the 5th and 15th percentile, the child is considered to be 'at risk' and it is recommended that the child is monitored carefully with special attention being paid to progress, particularly in activities that appear to cause difficulty.

Table A2.1 The 5th and 15th percentile points for the total scores on the Early Years Movement Skills Checklist.

Age	5th percentile	15th percentile
3	56	44
4	42	36
5	40	31

The table shows two useful cut-off scores for each age group. High Checklist scores indicate greater difficulties. The middle column shows the score that marks the boundary for the 5 per cent of the population with the most severe difficulties. Children achieving a total score at or above this level can be assumed to require more detailed assessment. The right-hand column shows the score for each age group that marks the boundary for the highest scoring 15 per cent of the population. Although it includes children with less severe difficulties than those identified by the 5 per cent scores, it represents children considered to be 'at risk' of movement difficulties.

Activities

Manual Activities

Activity 1

Equipment needed: 12 × 5p coins, 12 × 2p coins, empty 500ml water bottle with screw top.

a) Adult lays 2p coins 'Queen side' up on table in 4 rows. Child turns them over in place (don't slide them off the table). Time each hand.
b) Repeat with 5p coins.
c) Adult lays 2p coins on table – 4 rows 1" apart. Child holds bottle upright in one hand and posts coins in as fast as possible with other hand. Change hands. Time each.
d) Repeat with 5p coins.
e) Repeat (c) and (d) but don't touch top of bottle.
f) Child holds bottle with top screwed on containing 6 coins, on 'Go' child unscrews bottle and tips coins into non dominant hand them places them in 4 rows on table with dominant hand.
g) Repeat, changing hands.
h) Child holds bottle with top screwed on containing 6 coins, on 'Go' child unscrews bottle and tips coins into dominant hand then places them in rows on table with that hand (one handed placing).
i) Repeat with other hand.
j) Repeat (f), (g), (h) and (i) with 12 coins.

Activity 2

Equipment needed: pack of playing cards

a) Lay 12 cards flat on a table. Turn them over quickly, using one hand. Then change hands. Time each.
b) Lay 24 cards on a table. Time 2 hands turning cards – one in each hand.
c) Deal cards, holding the pack in one hand and dealing with the other. How many can you deal in one minute?
d) Hold 24 cards in one hand. Deal them using only one hand.
e) Repeat with the other hand.
f) Hold the whole pack in one hand. Deal using one hand only.
g) Teach child to shuffle the cards.
h) Play cards – teach the arrangement – in fan shape.

Activity 3: Bubble wrap pop

Equipment needed: bubble wrap

a) How many 'pincer pops' in one minute.

Activity 4: Pass the water bottle

Equipment needed: water bottle

a) Pass the water bottle hand to hand behind neck. Then behind waist. Time this.
b) Repeat the above with the water bottle full.
c) Pass heavier, awkward objects hand to hand round waist e.g. empty (but cold) hot water bottle – be inventive!

Activity 5: Peg power

Equipment needed: 13 pegs, wide necked jar.

a) Lay 12 pegs flat on table, unscrew jar and hold it steady with one hand. Using the remaining peg as 'tweezers', pick up the 12 pegs one by one and drop into jar.
b) Try with other objects.
c) Try with tweezers and spent matches.

Handwriting Activities

Activity 1: Spot the dot

Equipment needed: felt tip pen, *dotty paper (1)* and *(2)* (Figures A2.3 and A2.4)

a) Choose a felt tip pen and 'dot on dots' on *dotty paper (1)*. This must be done accurately – teach precision rather than speed at first.
b) Progress to *dotty paper (2)*, changing the colour of the felt tip pen.

Activity 2: Circles

Equipment needed: felt tip pen

a) Imitate drawing a circle – say 'round and stop'.
b) Child copies a circle
c) Practise drawing lots of circles – all different sizes.

Activity 3: Balloons

Equipment needed: felt tip pen, *balloon paper (1)* and *(2)* (Figures A2.5 and A2.6)

a) Draw over the balloons on *balloon paper (1)*, making sure that your lines are accurate.
b) Decorate with dots and stripes
c) Colour them in.
d) Draw your own balloons on *balloon paper (2)*.
e) Make the balloons all different colours.

Activity 4: Crosses

Equipment needed: felt tip pens, *cross paper* (Figure A2.7)

a) Imitate drawing a +. Parent to show how. Make both arms the same length. Practise if necessary.
b) Cover the *cross paper* with them. Make big and small crosses in lots of different colours.
c) Make sure the crosses don't touch and make sure that the lines are always straight.
d) When you have finished covering the page, find the best one.
e) On a new piece of paper, using one colour of felt tip, see how many crosses you can draw in one minute but be careful to still draw them accurately. Try to find someone that will compete with you and see who can draw the most in one minute.

Activity 5: Diagonals

Equipment needed: black pencil or felt tip pens, *It's raining paper (1)* and *(2)* (Figures A2.8 and A2.9)

a) On *It's raining paper (1)* make the rain really heavy by drawing over the lines with a black pencil of felt tip pen. Press hard on the paper.
b) Then do some smaller drops in between the bigger diagonals.
c) Colour the umbrella brightly to cheer you up. Draw over the spokes in a different colour.
d) Draw over the rain on *It's raining paper (2)*. Notice how the diagonals are going the other way. Do the same as for *It's raining paper (1)*.

Activity 6: Squares (1)

Equipment needed: felt tip pens, *squares paper (1)* (Figure A2.10)

a) Imitate drawing a square. It must have sharp corners.
b) Cover the *squares paper* with them. Make big and small squares in lots of different colours.
c) Make sure the squares don't touch and make sure that the lines are always straight.
d) When you have finished covering the page, find the best one.
e) On a new piece of paper, using one colour of felt tip, see how many squares you can draw in one minute but be careful to still draw them accurately. See if Mum or Dad will compete with you and see who can draw the most in one minute.

Activity 7: Squares (2)

Equipment needed: felt tip pens, *squares paper (2)* (Figure A2.11)

a) Cover the *squares paper (2)* with squares. Make the squares into presents by adding string and making sure that the cross stays inside the square.
b) Colour in the presents in lots of different colours.

Activity 8: Cross-kisses

Equipment needed: felt tip pens, *cross-kisses paper* (Figure A2.12)

a) Cover the *cross-kisses paper* with kisses. Make big and small kisses in lots of different colours.
b) Make sure the kisses don't touch and that the lines are always straight.
c) Notice the difference between crosses and kisses.

Activity 9: Triangles

Equipment needed: felt tip pens, *triangle trees paper*, *Christmas trees paper* (Figures A2.13 and A2.14)

a) Practise drawing triangles on a clean sheet of paper. Make sure that the triangles have 3 points. Make big and small triangles.
b) Make triangle trees on the *triangle trees paper*. Make lots of trees.
c) Make Christmas trees on the *Christmas trees paper*. Put presents on them (squares with cross inside).
d) Colour them in.

Activity 10: Shape combinations

Equipment needed: felt tip pens, *shape combination paper* (Figure A2.15)

a) Draw lots of shape combinations on the *shape combination paper*. Try to think of some of your own to draw.
b) Colour in the shapes in lots of different colours.

Dotty paper (1)

O   O   O   O   O   O   O

   O   O   O   O   O   O

O   O   O   O   O   O   O

   O   O   O   O   O   O

O   O   O   O   O   O   O

   O   O   O   O   O   O

O   O   O   O   O   O   O

   O   O   O   O   O   O

O   O   O   O   O   O   O

   O   O   O   O   O   O

O   O   O   O   O   O   O

   O   O   O   O   O   O

O   O   O   O   O   O   O

   O   O   O   O   O   O

O   O   O   O   O   O   O

   O   O   O   O   O   O

O   O   O   O   O   O   O

   O   O   O   O   O   O

O   O   O   O   O   O   O

  O   O   O   O   O   O
O   O   O   O   O   O   O

  O   O   O   O   O   O
O   O   O   O   O   O   O

  O   O   O   O   O   O
O   O   O   O   O   O   O

   O   O   O   O   O   O

Dotty paper (2)

Balloons (1)

Balloons (2)

Crosses paper

Cross-kisses

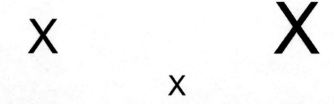

It's raining (1)

It's raining (2)

Squares (1)

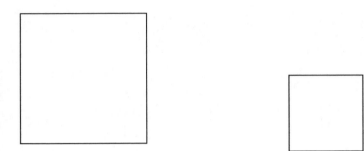

Squares (2)

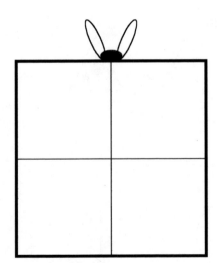

Triangle trees

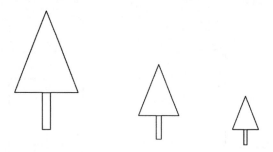

Christmas trees

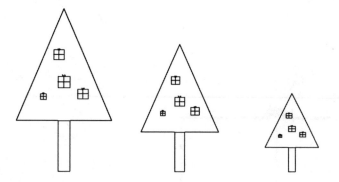

Shape combinations

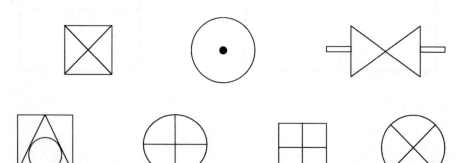

Balance Activities

Activity 1: Kneeling on all fours

Equipment needed: bean bag

a) Lift one straight arm forwards. Repeat with the other arm.
b) Straighten and lift one leg backwards (as high as possible). Repeat with the other leg.
c) Lift one leg (as above) and the opposite arm. Hold both and time it (don't slump!).
d) Repeat with the other arm and leg. Time this too.
e) Try with eyes closed.
f) Try with the bean bag balanced on head.

Activity 2: Standing

Equipment needed: bean bag

a) Pass the bean bag hand to hand round alternate lifted legs
b) Pass the bean bag hand to hand round lifted right leg (keep leg lifted). How many before over balancing?
c) Try with the left leg, then with eyes shut. Note the difference.

Activity 3: Standing balance

Equipment needed: masking tape

a) Make a 9 ft strip of 2 inch wide masking tape on the floor
b) Stand one foot in front of the other (heel touching toe). Time before over balancing. Then change forward foot.
c) Stand on tiptoe on tape (sideways with feet apart). Bring feet closer together till touching.
d) Stand as in (b) one foot in front of the other, but on tiptoe.
e) Stand with one foot along the tape and the other foot on top of the first (2nd foot mustn't touch the floor). Time to see how long child can stand like this.
f) Stand on one leg (one foot on the tape). How long can child stand like this?

NB. *Try all the activities for Activity 3 with eyes open and then with eyes closed.*

Activity 4: Moving balance at bottom stair

a) Step on/off the bottom stair (off backwards). How many times in one minute?
b) Run on and off backwards. Time it.
c) Jump on and off backwards. Time it.

Agility Activities

Activity 1: Heel–toe walking

Equipment needed: masking tape, bean bag

a) Place a long strip of masking tape on the floor.
b) Tiptoe walk along the masking tape (make sure each step is on the tape). Repeat this and balance the bean bag on head.
c) Heel–toe walk along the tape balancing bean bag on head.
d) Walk heel–toe and tiptoe backwards along the tape. Repeat this with the bean bag balanced on head.
e) Cross step over the tape. Repeat with the bean bag on head.

Activity 2: Jumping

Equipment needed: skipping rope, masking tape

a) Jump forwards and backwards over the tape.
b) Jump side to side over the tape.
c) Stride jump i.e. stand one foot each side of the tape and jump feet on to the tape then apart.
d) Stride jump – feet 'click' in the air over the tape then down to feet apart again.
e) Jump two feet together over rope. Gradually increase height.
f) Run and jump over the rope. Gradually increase height.

Activity 3: Hopping

Equipment needed: bean bag, masking tape

a) Stand with one foot on a bean bag. Slide bean bag forward. Step hop with other foot.
b) Change feet and repeat.
c) Hold two hands. Hop one foot on the spot. Repeat – hopping on other foot.

d) Hold one hand. Hop on one foot. Repeat – hopping on other foot.
e) Repeat without holding any hands.
f) Hop on the spot on the tape.
g) Hop forward and back over the tape.
h) Hop side to side over the tape.

Activity 4: Obstacle course

Equipment needed: skipping ropes, a bench or something similar, cones, masking tape, a blanket

a) Set up a short obstacle course consisting of ropes laid on the ground, strips of masking tape on the ground, cones etc. set out so the child has to weave in and out of them, a bench or something similar to run along, small obstacles for the child to jump over and a blanket laid flat for the child to crawl under.
b) Child to run slowly between the two ropes, hop along the masking tape, run in and out of the cones and along the bench, jump over the obstacles and crawl underneath the blanket.
c) Keep it fairly simple to begin with. As the child becomes more confident, make one or two activities more difficult, e.g. hopping side to side along the tape, standing jumps over the obstacles, vary the height of the obstacles
d) Vary the speed at which the child does the individual activities.
e) Change from one activity to another on command. Try to create smooth rather than jerky, stop–start actions.
f) With activities such as hopping and jumping ensure that there is a balanced beginning or ending.

Ball skills activities

Activity 1: Passing hand to hand

Equipment needed: rolled up jumper, sock roll, bean bag, tennis ball

a) Pass various objects round and round waist hand to hand in front, hand to hand behind.
b) Repeat passing objects round waist then round neck.
c) Try round alternate thigh, knee, ankle (keeping both feet on the floor).

NB. *Start with rolled jumper progressing to bean bag progressing to ball.*

Activity 2: Self-catch or throw–catch

Equipment needed: sock roll, bean bag, tennis ball

a) Child throws rolled jumper up a little way. Catch against body with 2 hands.
b) Try with (1) rolled sock; (2) bean bag; (3) tennis ball.
c) Try the above but catch away from the body.
d) Throw higher in the air.
e) Throw the tennis ball up, clap before catching. How many claps can the child do? Record number.
f) Child throws the tennis ball against a wall then (1) catches with 2 hands; (2) catches with 1 hand; (3) clap before catching. Try standing 3 ft away from wall, then 6 ft away, then 9 ft away.
g) Throw from under one knee or from behind back, turn round before catching etc. etc.

Activity 3: Bounce – catch

Equipment needed: tennis ball

a) Bounce tennis ball on floor and catch with 2 hands. Repeat activity but now catch with 1 hand. Practise catching with both hands separately.
b) Bounce ball to adult who catches it (1 hand bounce – 2 hand catch, then 1 hand bounce – 1 hand catch).
c) Child and adult stand each side of a sheet of A4 paper on the floor. Bounce the ball to each other, masking sure you hit the paper each time. Progress to half a sheet of paper, and gradually make the paper smaller. Count how many times you bounce the ball.

Activity 4: Catch thrown object (increasing distance)

Equipment needed: rolled jumper, rolled sock, bean bag, tennis ball

a) Start by catching the rolled jumper. Try catching against body at first. When 10 catches are successful try catching away from the body.
b) Repeat the above, catching (1) rolled sock; (2) bean bag; (3) tennis ball.
c) Repeat the above, but alternate what is thrown to the child, so the child doesn't know what is coming.

Try throwing from 3 ft, 4 ft, 6 ft, 9 ft and 12 ft. Rough measurement is fine. Make sure the child stands on a mat, so no cheating!

Activity 5: Advanced throw – catch

Equipment needed: rugby ball

a) Try with a rugby ball – try moving and catching. Play rugby.
b) Learn juggling.

Activity 6: Throwing: at target or power throw

Equipment needed: bean bag, washing up bowl, 12 screwed up pieces of A4 paper, football

a) Child stands on mat 4 ft from washing up bowl and throws bean bag into the bowl, using underarm action. Increase distance to 6 ft. Then try throwing bean bag to land on a smaller target (e.g. folded piece of A4 paper).
b) Put the washing up bowl on the floor and put 12 screwed up paper balls in the bowl. Child stands next to the bowl and throws the paper balls over arm as hard as possible to hit adult from 4 ft then 6 ft etc. Count number of hits.
c) Child and adult compete to throw paper balls as far and as hard as possible across the room. Train the child to stand with the opposite leg forward to the throwing arm.
d) Outside throwing practice. Throw the paper balls as far and hard as possible. Then practise hurling a football as far and hard as possible.

Activity 7: Bat and ball

Equipment needed: cardboard tube, balloon, large plastic bat, screwed up paper balls

a) Get child to hit a balloon with a cardboard tube. Start by getting the child to hit it when it is on the floor. When the child can do this throw the balloon for the child to hit with the cardboard tube.
b) Repeat the above using a large plastic bat and the screwed up paper balls.

References

American Psychiatric Association (1987) DSM-III-R Diagnostic and Statistical Manual of Mental Disorders. Washington DC: APA.

American Psychiatric Association (1994) DSM-IV Diagnostic and Statistical Manual of Mental Disorders. Washington DC: APA.

American Psychiatric Association (2000) DSM-IV-TR Diagnostic and Statistical Manual of Mental Disorders. Washington DC: APA.

Anning AJE (2003) Curriculum in the Early Years. Highlight No 197. National Children's Bureau/Barnados.

Apgar V (1953) A proposal for a new method of evaluation of the newborn infant. Current Researches in Anesthesia and Analgesia 32: 260–7.

Bard C, Fleury M, Carriere L et al. (1981) Components of the coincidence-anticipation behaviour of children aged from 6 to 16 years. Perceptual and Motor Skills 52: 547–56.

Bard C, Fleury M, Gagnon M (1990) Coincidence-anticipation timing: an age-related perspective. In C Bard, M Fleury, L Hay (eds), Developmental of Eye Hand Coordination across the Lifespan. Columbia SC: University of South Carolina Press.

Barkley RA (1998) (2nd edn) Attention Deficit Hyperactivity Disorder: A Handbook for Diagnosis and Treatment. New York: The Guilford Press.

Baron-Cohen S, Tager-Flusberg H, Cohen DJ (eds) (1993) Understanding Other Minds: Perspectives from Autism. Oxford: Oxford University Press.

Barnett A, Henderson SE (1992) Some observations on the figure drawings of clumsy children. British Journal of Educational Psychology 62: 341–55.

Barnett AL, Kooistra L, Henderson SE (eds) (1998) Clumsiness as syndrome and symptom. Human Movement Science 17: 435–47.

Bax M, Whitmore K (1987) The medical examination of children on entry to school. The results and use of neurodevelopmental assessment. Developmental Medicine and Child Neurology 29: 40–55.

Bayley N (1969a) Manual for the Bayley Scales of Infant Development. New York: The Psychological Corporation.

Bayley N (1969b) Bayley Scales of Infant Development. New York: The Psychological Corporation.

Bayley N (1993) (2nd edn) Bayley Scales of Infant Development. San Antonio, TX.: Therapy Skill Builders.

Bernheimer LP, Keogh BK (1995) Weaving interventions into the fabric of everyday life: an assessment to family assessment. Topics in Early Childhood Special Education 15: 415–33.

Bernstein N (1967) The Coordination and Regulation of Movement. New York: Pergamon Press.

Bishop DVM (1999) Uncommon Understanding. Hove: Psychology Press.

Blenkin G, Kelly AV (eds) (1997) Principles into Practice in Early Childhood Education. London: Paul Chapman.

Bowen JR, Gibson FL, Leslie GI et al. (1996) Predictive value of the Griffiths assessment in extremely low birthweight infants. Journal of Paediatrics and Child Health 32: 25–30.

Brenner MW, Gillman S (1966) Visuomotor ability in schoolchildren – a survey. Developmental Medicine and Child Neurology 8: 686–703.

Brenner MW, Gillman S, Zwangill OL et al. (1967) Visuomotor disability in school children. British Medical Journal 4: 259–62.

British Medical Journal (1962) Clumsy children. British Medical Journal 1665–6.

Burton AW, Miller DE (1998) Movement Skill Assessment. Champaign, IL.: Human Kinetics.

Cantell M, Smyth MM, Ahonen TP (1994) Clumsiness in adolescence: educational, motor and social outcomes of motor delay detected at 5 years. Adapted Physical Activity Quarterly 11: 115–29.

Chambers ME (2000) The Identification and Assessment of Young Children with Movement Difficulties. Unpublished doctoral dissertation, University of Leeds.

Chambers ME, Sugden DA (2002) The identification and assessment of young children with movement difficulties. International Journal of Early Years Education 10: 157–76.

Clark JE, Whitall J (1989) Changing patterns of locomotion: from walking to skipping. In MH Woollacott, A Shumway-Cook (eds), Development of Posture and Gait across the Lifespan. Columbia SC: University of South Carolina Press, pp. 128–51.

Cohen DJ, Volkmar FR (eds) (1997) Handbook of Autism and Pervasive Developmental Disorders (2nd edn). New York: John Wiley & Sons.

Connolly K, Elliott J (1972) The evolution and ontogeny of hand function. In NB Jones (ed.), Ethological Studies of Child Behaviour. Cambridge: Cambridge University Press.

Cratty BJ (1986) Perceptual and Motor Development in Infants and Children. Englewood Cliffs, NJ.: Prentice-Hall.

Dare MT, Gordon N (1970) Clumsy children: a disorder of perception and motor organisation. Developmental Medicine and Child Neurology 12: 178–85.

Department of Education and Employment (1999) Foundation Stage Curriculum for Under Fives. London: The Stationery Office.

Department for Education and Skills (2001) Special Educational Needs Code of Practice. Annesley: DfES.

Department for Education and Skills (2002) Birth to Three Matters. A framework for supporting children in the earliest years. London: The Stationery Office.

Dewey D, Kaplan BJ (1994) Subtyping of developmental motor deficits. Developmental Neuropsychology 10: 265–84.

Dewey D, Wilson BN, Crawford SG et al. (2000) Comorbidity of developmental coordination disorder with ADHD and reading disability. Journal of the International Neuropsychological Society 6: 152.

Dewey D, Kaplan BJ, Crawford SG et al. (2002) Developmental coordination disorder: associated problems in attention, learning, and psychosocial adjustment. Human Movement Science 21: 905–18.

Dorfman PW (1977) Timing and anticipation: a developmental perspective. Journal of Motor Behavior 9: 67–79.

Drillien C, Drummond M (1983) Development screening and the child with special needs. A population study of 5000 children. Clinics in Developmental Medicine, No. 86. London: SIMP with Heinemann Medical; Philadelphia: Lippincott.

Dwyer C, McKenzie B (1994) Impairment of visual memory in children who are clumsy. Adapted Physical Activity Quarterly 11: 179–89.

Edwards C, Gandini L, Forman G (1993) The Hundred Languages of Children: The Reggio Emilia Approach to Early Childhood Education. New Jersey: Ablex.

Espenschade AS, Eckert HM (1967) Motor Development. Colombus, Ohio: Charles Merrill Books.

Estil LB, Ingvaldsen RP, Whiting HTA (2002) Spatial and temporal constraints on performance in children with movement co-ordination problems. Experimental Brain Research 147: 153–61.

Flavell JH (1972) An analysis of cognitive developmental sequences. Genetic Psychology Monographs 86: 279–350.

Frankenburg WK, Dodds JB (1967) The Denver developmental screening test. Journal of Pediatrics 71: 181–91.

Frith U (2003) Autism: Explaining the Enigma (2nd ed). Oxford: Blackwell.

Gallahue DL (1982) Understanding Motor Development in Children. New York: John Wiley & Sons.

Gentile AM, Higgins JR, Miller EA et al. (1975) The structure of motor tasks. Movement 7: 11–28.

Gesell A (1928) Infancy and Human Growth. New York: Macmillan.

Gesell A (1946) The ontogenesis of infant behaviour. In L Carmichael (ed.), Manual of Child Psychology. New York: Wiley, pp. 295–331.

Geuze RH, Börger H (1993) Children who are clumsy. Adapted Physical Activity Quarterly 10: 10–21.

Geuze RH, Kalverboer AF (1994) Tapping a rhythm: a problem of timing for children who are clumsy and dyslexic? Adapted Physical Activity Quarterly 11: 203–13.

Gibson JJ, Gibson EJ (1979) The Perception of the Visual World. Boston: Houghton Mifflin.

Gillberg C (1983) Perceptual, motor and attentional deficits in Swedish primary school children: some child psychiatric aspects. Journal of Child Psychology and Psychiatry 24: 377–403.

Gillberg C (1998) Hyperactivity, inattention and motor control problems: prevalence, comorbidity and background factors. Folia Phoniatrica et Logopaedica 50: 107–17.

Gillberg C, Rasmussen P (1982a) Perceptual, motor and attentional deficits in six-year-old children: Screening procedure in pre-school. Acta Paediatrica Scandinavica 71: 121–9.

Gillberg C, Rasmussen P (1982b) Perceptual, motor and attentional deficits in seven-year-old children: Background factors. Developmental Medicine and Child Neurology 24: 752–70.

Gillberg C, Kadesjö B (1998) Attention deficit/hyperactivity disorder and developmental coordination disorder. In TE Brown (ed.), Attention Deficit Disorders and Comorbidities in Children, Adolescents and Adults. Washington, DC: American Psychiatric Press, pp. 393–406.

Gillberg C, Coleman M (2000) The Biology of the Autistic Syndromes. London: MacKeith.

Gillberg C, Kadesjö B (2000) Attention-deficit/hyperactivity disorder and developmental coordination disorder. In TE Brown (ed.), Attention-deficit Disorders and Comorbidities in Children, Adolescents and Adults. Washington DC: American Psychiatric Press.

Gillberg C, Rasmussen P, Carlström G et al. (1982) Perceptual, motor and attentional deficits in six-year-old children: epidemiological aspects. Journal of Child Psychology and Psychiatry 23: 131–44.

Gillberg IC (1985) Children with minor neurodevelopmental disorders III: Neurological and neurodevelopmental problems at age 10. Developmental Medicine and Child Neurology 27: 3–16.

Gillberg IC, Gillberg C (1983) Three years follow-up at age 10 of children with minor neurodevelopmental disorders. I: Behavioural problems. Developmental Medicine and Child Neurology 25: 438–49.

Gillberg IC, Gillberg C (1989) Children with preschool minor neurodevelopmental disorders. IV: Behavioural and school achievement at age 13. Developmental Medicine and Child Neurology 31: 3–13.

Gillberg IC, Gillberg C, Groth J (1989) Children with preschool minor neurodevelopmental disorders V: Neurodevelopmental profiles at age 13. Developmental Medicine and Child Neurology 31: 14–24.

Glascoe FP (2001) Are overreferrals on developmental screening test really a problem? Archives of Pediatric and Adolescent Medicine 155: 54–9.

Goldfield EC (1995) Emergent Forms: Origins and Early Development of Human Action and Perception. New York: Oxford University Press.

Goldfield EC, Wolff PH (2004) A dynamical systems perspective on infant development. In G Bremner, A Slater (eds) Theories of Infant Development. Oxford: Blackwell, pp. 3–29.

Griffiths R (1967) Griffiths Mental Development Scales for Testing Babies and Young Children from Birth to Eight Years of Age. Amersham, Bucks: Association of Research in Infant Development.

Gubbay SS (1975a) The Clumsy Child. London: Saunders & Co.

Gubbay SS (1975b) Clumsy children in normal schools. The Medical Journal of Australia 1: 233–6.

Gubbay SS, Ellis E, Walton JN et al. (1965) Clumsy children: a study of apraxic and agnosic defects in 21 children. Brain 88: 295–312.

Hall DMB (1988) Clumsy children. British Medical Journal 296: 375–6.

Hall A, McCleod A, Counsell C et al. (1995) School attainment, cognitive ability and motor function in a Scottish very low birthweight population at eight years: a controlled study. Developmental Medicine and Child Neurology 37: 1037–50.

Halverson HM (1931) An experimental study of prehension in infants by means of systematic cinema records. Genetic Psychology Monographs 10: 107–286.

Haley SM, Coster WJ, Ludlow LH et al. (1992) Pediatric Evaluation of Disability Inventory (PEDI). Boston: New England Medical Center Hospitals.

Haywood KM (1993) Lifespan Motor Development. Champaign, IL.: Human Kinetics.

Haywood KM, Getchell N (2001) Lifespan Motor Development (3rd edn). Champaign IL.: Human Kinetics.

Hellgren L, Gillberg C, Gillberg IC et al. (1993) Children with deficits in attention, motor control and perception (DAMP) almost grown up. General health at age 16 years. Developmental Medicine and Child Neurology 35: 881–92.

Henderson L, Rose P, Henderson SE (1992) Reaction time and movement time in children with a developmental coordination disorder. Journal of Child Psychology and Psychiatry 33: 895–905.

Henderson SE (1987) The assessment of 'clumsy' children: old and new approaches. Journal of Child Psychology and Psychiatry 28: 511–27.

Henderson SE (1992) Clumsiness or developmental coordination disorder: a neglected handicap. Current Paediatrics 2:158–62.

Henderson SE (1994) Editorial. Adapted Physical Activity Quarterly 11: 111–14.

Henderson SE, Hall D (1982) Concomitants of clumsiness in young schoolchildren. Developmental Medicine and Child Neurology 24: 448–60.

Henderson SE, May DS, Umney M (1989) An exploratory study of goal-setting behaviour, self-concept and locus of control in children with movement difficulties. European Journal of Special Needs Education 4: 1–15.

Henderson SE, Sugden DA (1992) Movement Assessment Battery for Children. London: The Psychological Corporation.

Hill E (2001) Non-specific nature of specific language impairment: a review of the literature with regard to concomitant motor impairments. International Journal of Language and Communication Disorders 36: 149–71.

Hinshaw SP (1994) Attention Deficits and Hyperactivity in Children. Thousand Oaks, CA: Sage Publications.

Hoare D (1994) Subtypes of developmental coordination disorder. Adapted Physical Activity Quarterly 11: 158–69.

Hulme C, Biggerstaff A, Moran G et al. (1982a) Visual, kinaesthetic and cross-modal judgements of length by normal and clumsy children. Developmental Medicine and Child Neurology 24: 461–71.

Hulme C, Smart A, Moran G (1982b) Visual perceptual deficits in clumsy children. Neuropsychologica 20: 475–81.

Hulme C, Smart A, Moran G et al. (1984) Visual, kinaesthetic and cross-modal judgements of length by clumsy children: a comparison with young normal children. Child: Care, Health and Development 10: 117–25.

Hulme C, Snowling M (eds) (1997) Dyslexia: Biology, Cognition and Intervention. London: Whurr.

Iloeje SE (1987) Developmental apraxia among Nigerian children in Enugu, Nigeria. Developmental Medicine and Child Neurology 29: 502–7.

Jongmans MJ (2005) Early identification of children with developmental coordination disorder. In DA Sugden, ME Chambers (eds) (2005) Children with Developmental Coordination Disorder. London: Whurr.

Jordan R (1999) Autistic Spectrum Disorders. London: David Fulton.

Kadesjö B, Gillberg C (1999a) Attention deficits and clumsiness in Swedish 7-year-old children. Developmental Medicine and Child Neurology 40: 796–804.

Kadesjö B, Gillberg C (1999b) Developmental coordination disorder in Swedish 7-year-old children. Journal of American Academy of Child and Adolescent Psychiatry 38: 820–8.

Kalverboer AF (1988) Hyperactivity and observational studies. In LN Bloomingdale, JA Sergeant (eds), Attention Deficit Disorder: Criteria, Cognition, and Intervention, Vol. 5. Oxford: Pergamon.

Kalverboer AF, Hopkins B, Geuze R (eds) (1993) Motor Development in Early and Later Childhood: Longitudinal Approaches. London: University Press.

Kaplan BJ, Wilson BN, Dewey D et al. (1998) DCD may not be a discrete disorder. Human Movement Science 17: 471–90.

Kaplan B, Dewey D, Crawford S et al. (2001) The term comorbidity is of questionable value in reference to developmental disorders: data and theory. Journal of Learning Disabilities 34: 555–65.

Kavale KA, Nye C (1985–1986) Parameters of learning disabilities in achievement, linguistic, neuropsychological, and social/behavioural domains. Journal of Special Education 19: 443-58.

Keogh JF (1968) Developmental evaluation of limb movement tasks. Technical report 1-68 (USPHS Grant HD 01059). Los Angeles: Department of Physical Education, University of California.

Keogh JF (1969) Analysis of limb and body control tasks. Technical report 1-69 (USPHS Grant HD 01059). Los Angeles: Department of Physical Education, University of California.

Keogh JF, Sugden DA (1985) Movement Skill Development. New York, NY: Macmillan.

Keogh JF, Sugden DA, Reynard CL et al. (1979) Identification of clumsy children: Comparisons and comments. Journal of Human Movement Studies 5: 32–51.

Kirby A, Davies R (in preparation) Is crawling a motor milestone that is important in children with DCD?

Kirby A, Davies R, Harris A (in preparation) Health and educational professional awareness of specific learning difficulties-is there a need for training?

Klin A, Carter A, Volkmar FR et al. (1997) Developmentally based assessments. In DJ Cohen, FR Volkmar (eds), Handbook of Autism and Pervasive Developmental Disorders (2nd edn). New York: John Wiley & Sons, pp. 411–47.

Knight E, Henderson SE, Losse A et al. (1992) Clumsy at six – still clumsy at sixteen: the educational and social consequences of having motor difficulties at school. In T Williams, L Almond, A Sparkes (eds), Sport and Physical Activity: Moving towards Excellency. London: Chapman & Hall, pp. 249–59.

Knobloch H, Pasamanick B (eds) (1974) Gesell and Armatruda's Developmental Diagnosis (3rd edn). New York: Harper & Row.

Koegel RL, Koegel LK (eds) (1996) Teaching Children with Autism. Baltimore, Maryland: Paul H. Brookes Publishing Co.

Kugler P, Turvey M (1987) Information, Natural Law and the Self Assembly of Rhythmic Movements. Hillsdale, NJ: Erlbaum.

Laszlo JI, Bairstow P (1985) Perceptual-motor Behaviour: Development, Assessment and Therapy. London: Holt, Rinehart & Winston.

Laszlo JI, Bairstow PJ, Bartrip J (1988a) A new approach to treatment of perceptuo-motor dysfunction: previously called 'clumsiness'. Support for Learning 3: 35–40.

Laszlo JI, Bairstow PJ, Bartrip J et al. (1988b) Clumsiness or perceptuo-motor dysfunction? In A Colley, J Beech (eds), Cognition and Action in Skilled Behaviour. Amsterdam: North-Holland, pp. 293–316.

Lefebvre C, Reid G (1998) Prediction in ball catching with and without developmental coordination disorder. Adapative Physical Activity Quarterly 15: 299–315.

Lord R, Hulme C (1987a) Perceptual judgements of normal and clumsy children. Developmental Medicine and Child Neurology 29: 250–7.

Lord R, Hulme C (1987b) Kinaesthetic sensitivity of normal and clumsy children. Developmental Medicine and Child Neurology 29: 720–5.

Lord R, Hulme C (1988) Patterns of rotary pursuit performance in clumsy and normal children. Journal of Child Psychology and Psychiatry 29: 691–701.

Losse A, Henderson SE, Elliman D et al. (1991) Clumsiness in children – do they grow out of it? A 10-year follow up study. Developmental Medicine and Child Neurology 33: 55–68.

Luiz DM, Foxcroft CD, Stewart R (2001) The construct validity of the Griffiths Scales of Mental Development. Child: Care, Health and Development 27: 73–83.

Lyytinen H, Ahonen T (1989) Motor precursors of learning disabilities. In DJ Bakker, Van der Vlugt (eds), Learning Disabilities: Vol. 1. Neuropsychological Correlates. Amsterdam: Swets & Zeitlinger, pp. 35–43.

McGovern R (1991) Developmental dyspraxia: or just plain clumsy? Early Years 12: 37–8.

McGraw MB (1932) From reflex to muscular control in the assumption of an erect posture and ambulation in the human infant. Child Development 3: 291–7.

McGraw MB (1963) The Neuromuscular Maturation of the Human Infant (reprint edn). New York: Columbia University Press.

Macnab JJ, Miller LT, Polatajko HJ (2001) The search for subtypes of DCD: is cluster analysis the answer? Human Movement Science 20: 49–72.

Maeland AF (1992) Identification of children with motor coordination problems. Adapted Physical Activity Quarterly 9: 330–42.

Maude P (2003) Observing Children Moving. United Kingdom: Physical Education Association.

Michaelson K, Lindhal E (1993) Relationship between perinatal risk factors and motor development at the ages of 5 and 9 years. In AF Kalverboer, B Hopkins, R Geuze (eds), Motor Development in Early and Later Childhood: Longitudinal Approaches. Cambridge, UK: Cambridge University Press, pp. 266–85.

Ministry of Education, New Zealand (1996) Te Whariki. Wellington: New Zealand Learning Media.

Missiuna C (1994) Motor skill acquisition in children with developmental coordination disorder. Adapted Physical Activity Quarterly 11: 214–35.

Miyahara M (1994) Subtypes of students with learning disabilities based upon gross motor functions. Adapted Physical Activities Quarterly 11: 368–82.

Miyahara M, Möbs I (1995) Developmental dyspraxia and developmental coordination disorder. Neuropsychology Review 5: 245–68.

Mon-Williams MA, Pascal E, Wann JP (1994) Ophthalmic factors in developmental coordination disorder. Adapted Physical Activity Quarterly 11: 170–8.

Newell KM (1986) Constraints on the development of coordination. In MG Wade, HTA Whiting (eds), Motor Development in Children: Aspects of Coordination and Control. Dordrecht, Netherlands: Nijhoff, pp. 341–60.

Newell KM, Scully DM, Macdonald PV et al. (1989a) Task constraints and infant grip configuration. Developmental Psychobiology 22: 817–31.

Newell KM, Tenebaum F, Hardiman S (1989b) Bodyscale and the development of prehension. Developmental Psychobiology 22: 1–13.

Nichols PL, Chen TC (1981) Minimal Brain Dysfunction: A Prospective Study. Hillsdale, NJ.: Erlbaum.

O'Beirne C, Larkin D, Cable T (1994) Coordination problems and anaerobic performance in children. Adapted Physical Activity Quarterly 11: 141–9.

O'Hare A, Khalid S (2002) The association of abnormal cerebellar function in children with developmental coordination disorder and reading difficulties. Dyslexia 8: 234–48.

Orton ST (1937) Reading, Writing and Speech Problems in Children. New York: Norton.

Piaget J (1952) The Origins of Intelligence in Children. New York: International Universities Press.

Polatajko HJ, Fox M, Missiuna C (1995a) An international consensus on children with developmental coordination disorder. Canadian Journal of Occupational Therapy 62: 3–6.

Polatajko HJ, Macnab JJ, Anstett B et al. (1995b) A clinical trial of the process-oriented treatment approach for children with developmental coordination disorder. Developmental Medicine and Child Neurology 37: 310–19.

Polatajko HJ, Mandich A, Miller L (2001a) Cognitive orientation to occupational performance (CO-OP): Part II – The evidence. Physical and Occupational Therapy in Pediatrics 20: 83–106.

Polatajko HJ, Mandich A, Missiuna C et al. (2001b) Cognitive orientation to daily occupational performance (CO-OP): Part III – The protocol in brief. Physical and Occupational Therapy in Pediatrics 20: 107–24.

Prizant BM, Schuler AL, Wetherby AM (1997) Enhancing language and communication development: language approaches. In DJ Cohen, FR Volkmar (eds), Handbook of Autism and Pervasive Developmental Disorders (2nd edn). New York: John Wiley & Sons, pp. 572–605.

Roberton MA (1977) Stability of stage categorizations across trials: implications for the 'stage theory' of overarm throw development. Journal of Human Movement Studies 3: 49–59.

Roberton MA (1978) Longitudinal evidence for developmental stages in the forceful overarm throw. Journal of Human Movement Studies 4: 167–75.

Roberton MA (1984) Changing motor patterns during childhood. In JR Thomas (ed.), Motor Development during Childhood and Adolescence. Burgess, Minneapolis, pp. 48–90.

Rösblad B, von Hofsten C (1994) Repetitive goal-directed arm movements in children with developmental coordination disorders: role of visual information. Adapted Physical Activity Quarterly 11: 190–202.

Roth SC, Baudin J, Pezzani-Goldsmith M et al. (1994) Relation between neurodevelopmental status of very preterm infants at one and eight years. Developmental Medicine and Child Neurology 36: 1049–62.

Roussounis SH, Gaussen TH, Stratton P (1987) A 2-year follow up of children with motor coordination problems identified as school entry age. Child: Care, Health and Development 13: 377–91.

Sassoon R (1990) Handwriting: The Way to Teach It. Cheltenham: Stanley Thornes.

Sassoon R (2003) Handwriting: The Way to Teach It (2nd edn). London: Paul Chapman Educational Publishing.

Schmidt RA (1991) Motor Learning and Performance. Champagne, IL.: Human Kinetics.

Schmidt RA, Lee TD (1999) Motor Control and Learning. Champaign, IL.: Human Kinetics.

Schoemaker MM, Kalverboer AF (1994) Social and affective problems of children who are clumsy: how early do they begin? Adapted Physical Activity Quarterly 11: 130–40.

Schoemaker MM, Hijlkema MGJ, Kalverboer AF (1994) Physiotherapy for clumsy children – an evaluation study. Developmental Medicine and Child Neurology 36: 143–55.

Schoemaker MM, Wees M, van der Flapper B et al. (2001) Perceptual skills of children with developmental coordination disorder. Human Movement Science 20: 111–33.

Schuler AL, Prizant BM, Wetherby AM (1997) Enhancing language and communication development: prelinguistic approaches in DJ Cohen, FR Volkmar (eds), Handbook of Autism and Pervasive Developmental Disorders (2nd edn). New York: John Wiley & Sons, pp. 539–71.

Shirley MM (1931) The First Two Years: A Study of Twenty-Five Babies. Vol. 1: Postural and Locomotor Development. Minneapolis: University of Minnesota Press.

Sigmundsson H, Hansen PC, Talcott JB (2003) Do 'clumsy' children have visual deficits? Behavioural Brain Research 139: 123–9.

Silver AA, Hagin RA (1990) Disorders of Learning in Childhood. New York: John Wiley & Sons.

Sims K, Henderson SE, Hulme C et al. (1996a) The remediation of clumsiness: I. An evaluation of Laszlo's kinaesthetic approach. Developmental Medicine and Child Neurology 38: 976–87.

Sims K, Henderson SE, Morton J et al. (1996b) The remediation of clumsiness: II. Is kinaesthesis the answer? Developmental Medicine and Child Neurology 38: 988–97.

Skinner RA, Piek JP (2001) Psychosocial implications of poor motor coordination in children and adolescents. Human Movement Science 20:73–94.

Skorji V, McKenzie B (1997) How do children who are clumsy remember modelled movements? Developmental Medicine and Child Neurology 39: 404–8.

Smoll FL (1973) A rhythmic ability analysis system. Research Quarterly 44: 232–6.

Smyth MM, Mason UC (1997) Planning and execution of action in children with and without developmental coordination disorder. Journal of Child Psychology and Psychiatry 38: 1023-37.

Smyth MM, Anderson H (2000) Coping with clumsiness in the school playground: social and physical play in children with co-ordination impairments. British Journal of Developmental Psychology 18: 389–413.

Smyth TR, Glencross DJ (1986) Information processing deficits in clumsy children. Australian Journal of Psychology 38: 13–22.

Snowling MJ (2000) (2nd edn) Dyslexia. Malden, MA.: Blackwell Publishers.

Stanley F, Alberman E (1984) Birthweight, gestational age and the cerebral palsies. In F Stanley, E Alberman (eds), The Epidemiology of the Cerebral Palsies. London: Spastics International, pp. 135–49.

Stephenson E, McKay C, Chesson R (1991) The identification and treatment of motor/learning difficulties: parents' perceptions and the role of the therapist. Child: Care, Health and Development 17: 91–113.

Sugden DA (in press) Dynamic management of developmental coordination disorder. In R Geuze (ed.) La Maladress chez les Enfants Persentant un Trouble d'acquisition des Coordination Motrices: Revue des approaches actuelles. (Developmental coordination disorder: a review of current approaches.)

Sugden DA, Wann C (1987) The assessment of motor impairment in children with moderate learning difficulties. British Journal of Educational Psychology 57: 225–36.

Sugden DA, Keogh JF (1990) Problems in Movement Skill Development. Columbia: University of South Carolina Press.

Sugden DA, Sugden L (1991) The assessment of movement skill problems in 7- and 9-year old children. British Journal of Educational Psychology 61: 329–45.

Sugden DA, Henderson SE (1994) Help with movement. Special Children 75: Back to Basics 13.

Sugden DA, Utley A (1995) Interlimb coupling in children with hemiplegic cerebral palsy. Developmental Medicine and Child Neurology 37: 293–310.

Sugden DA, Wright HC (1996) Curricular entitlement and implementation for all children. In N. Armstrong (ed.), New Directions in Physical Education: Vol. 3. Change and Innovation. London: Cassells, pp. 110–30.

Sugden DA, Chambers ME (1998) Intervention approaches and children with developmental coordination disorder. Pediatric Rehabilitation 2: 139–47.

Sugden DA, Wright HC (1998) Motor Coordination Disorders in Children. Thousand Oaks, CA: Sage Publications.

Sugden DA, Chambers ME (2003) Intervention in children with developmental coordination disorder: the role of parents and teachers. British Journal of Educational Psychology 73: 545–61.

Sugden DA, Chambers ME (2005) Children with Developmental Coordination Disorder. London: Whurr.

Thelen E (1985) Developmental origins of motor coordination: leg movements in human infants. Developmental Psychobiology 18: 1–22.

Thelen E (1986) Development of coordinated movement: implications for early human development. In MG Wade, HTA Whiting (eds), Movement Development in Children: Aspects of Coordination and Control. Boston: Martinus Nijhoff, pp. 107–24.

Thelen E (1995) Motor development: a new synthesis. American Psychologist 50: 79–95.

Thelen E, Fisher DM (1982) Newborn stepping: an explanation for a 'disappearing reflex'. Developmental Psychology 18: 760–75.

Thelen E, Fisher DM (1983) The organization of spontaneous leg movements in newborn infants. Journal of Motor Behavior 15: 353–77.

Thelen E, Ulrich BD (1991) Hidden skills: a dynamic systems analysis of treadmill stepping during the first year. Society for Research in Child Development Monographs 56: 1–98.

Thelen E, Smith LB (1994) A Dynamic Systems Approach to the Development of Cognition and Action. Cambridge MA: MIT Press.

Thelen E, Ridley-Johnson R, Fisher DM (1983) Shifting patterns of bilateral coordination and lateral dominance in the leg movements of young infants. Developmental Psychobiology 15: 447–53.

Tomblin JB, Records NL, Buckwalter P et al. (1997) The prevalence of specific language impairment in kindergarten children. Journal of Speech, Language, and Hearing Research 40: 1245–60.

Ulrich BD (1997) Dynamic systems theory and skill development in infants and children. In KJ Connolly, H Forssberg (eds), Neurophysiology and Neuropsychology of Motor Development. Clinics in Developmental Medicine No. 143/144. London: MacKeith Press, pp. 319–45.

Utley A, Sugden DA (1998) Interlimb coupling in children with hemiplegic cerebral palsy during reaching and grasping at speed. Developmental Medicine and Child Neurology 40: 396–404.

Vaessen W, Kalverboer AF (1990) Clumsy children's performance on a double task. In AF Kalverboer (ed.), Developmental Biopsychology: Experimental and Observational Studies in Children at Risk. Ann Arbor: University of Michigan Press, pp. 223–40.

van Dellen T, Geuze RH (1988) Motor response processing in clumsy children. Journal of Child Psychology and Psychiatry 29: 489–500.

van Dellen T, Geuze RH (1990) Experimental studies on motor control in clumsy children. In AF Kalverboer (ed.), Developmental Biopsychology: Experimental and Observational Studies in Children at Risk. Ann Arbor: University of Michigan Press, pp. 187–205.

van der Kamp J, Savelsbergh GJP, Davis WE (1998) Body-scaled ratio as a control parameter for prehension in 5 to 9 year old children. Developmental Psychobiology 33: 351–61.

van der Meulen JHP, Denier van de Gon JJ, Gielen CCAM et al. (1991) Visuomotor performance of normal and clumsy children II: Arm-tracking movements with and without visual feedback. Developmental Medicine and Child Neurology 33: 118–29.

Visser J (2003) Developmental coordination disorder: a review of research on subtypes and comorbidities. Human Movement Science 22: 479–93.

Wade MG (1980) Coincidence anticipation of young normal and handicapped children. Journal of Motor Behavior 12: 103–12.

Walton JN, Ellis E, Court SDM (1962) Clumsy children: developmental apraxia and agnosia. Brain 85: 603–12.

Wann JP (1987) Trends in the refinement and optimization of fine-motor trajectories: Observations from an analysis of the handwriting of primary school children. Journal of Motor Behavior 19: 13–37.

Wender PH (2000) ADHD: Attention-deficit hyperactivity disorder in children, adolescents, and adults. Oxford: Oxford University Press.

Wetherby AM, Schuler AL, Prizant BM (1997) Enhancing language and communication development: theoretical foundations. In DJ Cohen, FR Volkmar (eds), Handbook of Autism and Pervasive Developmental Disorders (2nd edn). New York: John Wiley & Sons, pp. 513–38.

Williams HG (1973) Perceptual-motor development in children. In CB Corbin (ed.), A Textbook of Motor Development. Dubuque, Ia.: William C Brown.

Wilson JR (1998) The Hand. New York: Pantheon.

Wilson P, McKenzie B (1998) Information processing deficits associated with developmental coordination disorder: a meta-analysis of research findings. Journal of Child Psychology and Psychiatry 39: 829–40.

Wing AM, Haggard P, Flanagan R (eds) (1996) Hand and Brain: The Neurophysiology and Psychology of Hand Movements. San Diego: Academic Press.

World Health Organization (1992a) International Statistical Classification of Diseases and Related Health Problems. Tenth Edition Volume 1 ICD-10. Geneva: World Health Organization.

World Health Organization (1992b) Classification of Mental and Behavioural Disorders: Clinical descriptions and diagnostic guidelines. Geneva: World Health Organization.

World Health Organization (1993) Classification of Mental and Behavioural Disorders – Diagnostic criteria for research. Geneva: World Health Organization.

World Health Organization (2001) International Classification of Functioning, Disability and Health (ICF). Geneva: World Health Organization.

Wright HC (1996) The Identification, Assessment and Management of Children with Developmental Coordination Disorder. Unpublished doctoral thesis. University of Leeds.

Wright HC, Sugden DA (1996a) A two-step procedure for the identification of children with developmental coordination disorder in Singapore. Developmental Medicine and Child Neurology 38: 1099–1105.

Wright HC, Sugden DA (1996b) The nature of developmental coordination disorder: Inter- and intragroup differences. Adapted Physical Activity Quarterly 13: 357–71.

Wright HC, Sugden DA (1996c) The nature of developmental coordination disorder in children aged 6–9 years of age. Journal of Sports Sciences 14: 50–1.

Wright HC, Sugden DA (1998) A school based intervention programme for children with developmental coordination disorder. European Journal of Physical Education 3: 35–50.

Wright HC, Sugden DA (1999) Physical Education for All. London: David Fulton.

Wright HC, Sugden DA, Ng R, Tan J (1994) Identification of children with movement problems in Singapore: Usefulness of the Movement ABC Checklist. Adapted Physical Activity Quarterly 11: 150–7.

Zelazo PR, Zelazo NA, Kolb S (1972a) Walking in the newborn. Science 176: 314–15.

Zelazo PR, Zelazo NA, Kolb S (1972b) Newborn walking. Science 177: 1058–9 (letter).

Index